943

E
Canary
Islands

by

ADAM HOPKINS

and

GABRIELLE MACPHEDRAN

Adam Hopkins is a travel writer and regular
contributor to the *Daily Telegraph* and *Sunday Times.*
He is the author of *Essential Riviera* and *Essential Crete*,
and has written books on Crete and Holland.

Gabrielle Macphedran is a journalist and broadcaster.

Produced by AA Publishing

Written by Adam Hopkins and
Gabrielle Macphedran
Peace and Quiet section
by Paul Sterry

Edited, designed and produced
by AA Publishing. Maps ©
The Automobile Association
1994

Distributed in the United
Kingdom
by AA Publishing, Fanum
House,
Basingstoke, Hampshire,
RG21 2EA.

The contents of this publication
are believed correct at the time
of printing. Nevertheless, the
publishers cannot be held
responsible for any errors or
omissions, or for changes in
details given in this guide or for
the consequences of any
reliance on the information
provided by the same.
Assessments of attractions,
hotels, restaurants and so forth
are based upon the author's
own experience and, therefore,
descriptions given in this guide
necessarily contain an element
of subjective opinion which
may not reflect the publisher's
opinion or dictate a reader's
own experience on another
occasion.
**We have tried to ensure
accuracy in this guide, but
things do change and we
would be grateful if readers
would advise us of any
inaccuracies they may
encounter.**

First edition published 1991
Revised Second edition © The
Automobile Association 1994

A CIP catalogue record for this
book is available from the
British Library.

ISBN 0 7495 0834 5

Published by AA Publishing,
which is a trading name of
Automobile Association
Developments Limited, whose
registered office is Fanum
House, Basingstoke,
Hampshire,
RG21 2EA.
Registered number 1878835.

Colour separation: BTB Colour
Reproduction, Whitchurch,
Hampshire

Printed by: Printers Trento,
S.R.L., Italy

Front cover picture: *Tenerife*

CONTENTS

This book employs a simple rating system to help choose which places to visit:

✓	'top ten'

◆◆◆	do not miss
◆◆	see if you can
◆	worth seeing if you have time

INTRODUCTION

The Canary Islands lie not far north of the Tropic of Cancer and close to the shoulder of Saharan Africa. They are the nearest place to Northern Europe with real hope of winter sun. The summer climate is milder than one might expect, hot but pleasurable. It is this outstanding climate, potentially offering a year-round season, which has been the Canaries' fortune and misfortune. Booming tourism in the 1960s and 1970s led to the construction of colossal and still-growing resorts in the two largest islands, Tenerife and Gran Canaria (the latter perhaps better known under the name of its capital city, Las Palmas.) These two destinations are certainly familiar to all readers of holiday advertisements, their resorts much loved by some and abominated by others. Recently the smaller, volcanic island of Lanzarote has joined the tourist listings in a big way.

The pity of it is that those who do not know the Canaries believe the mass holiday phenomenon is the whole story. In fact, the seven Canary

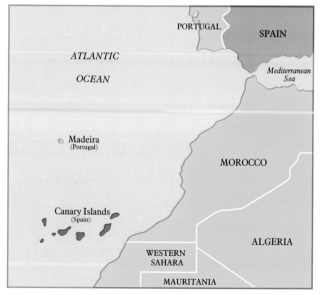

Prickly pears were first grown in the Canaries as an important crop, but many now grow semi-wild

Islands and their lesser islets offer astonishing physical variety and scenes of the greatest natural beauty, by turns savage and peaceful, and ranging in vegetation from the lushest greenery to outright desert. Even the islands with the biggest number of visitors retain large tracts of untroubled countryside, sometimes given over to vines, bananas and other tropical produce but even more often wild and mountainous. Some of the islands, unbelievably, are virtually untouched by tourism.

Basically, there are two groups. The eastern islands are Gran Canaria, Lanzarote and Fuerteventura lying close to Africa. Then there are the western islands, Tenerife, Gomera, Hierro and La Palma (not to be confused with Las Palmas), riding a little further out into the Atlantic Ocean.

Of the first group, Gran Canaria/Las Palmas has on its southern side the biggest seaside resort in the whole of Spain and her possessions – not excluding Benidorm and the Costa Brava. This is both a plus and a minus. Lanzarote, now becoming very popular, is a moonscape of craters and volcanoes, one at least – Timanfaya, the Mountain of Fire – still impressively active. Fuerteventura is a desert island, barren and strange and ringed by brilliant beaches.

INTRODUCTION

Of the outer group, Tenerife is the largest. In fact, it is considerably the biggest of all the Canary Islands. The individual resorts, however, are just a little smaller than those on Las Palmas, though they do exist on both the north and south sides of the island. In the middle stands Spain's highest mountain, the vast volcanic cone of Teide, surrounded on all sides by high and lovely country. Tenerife is certainly an island of extremes. But it is the tiny islands out to the west again which are perhaps the most extraordinary, true gems of the Atlantic Ocean. La Palma and Gomera in particular remain to this day genuinely unspoilt. Both are strange and lofty, astonishingly beautiful, not so wonderful for swimming but ideal for lovers of nature, for walkers and for those in search of unhassled relaxation.

The fact is that the Canaries offer an island for every taste, whether the preference is for solitude or cheerful, gregarious holidays. The trick is to think carefully in advance and choose the island most suitable for you. The result may very well be enchantment.

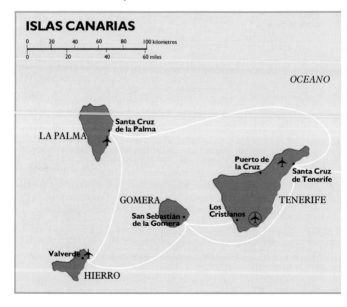

BACKGROUND

The Canaries have been known to Europe, though very vaguely, since the dawn of recorded history. The Greeks called them the Fortunate Islands and some have been pleased to link them with the lost continent of Atlantis. From long before recorded history, however, and right up to the 15th century AD, they were inhabited by a simple, vigorous people of unknown origins, the Guanches. Conquest by Spain devastated their communities and civilisation. Now the islands are truly Spanish, peopled by Spaniards intermingled with the last remnants of the Guanches. They are administered, in two provinces, as if they were part of mainland Spain. Like other large regions of Spain, they now enjoy a degree of local autonomy.

In the early days of Spanish rule, the agriculture of the islands produced enough food for the limited population. Later, the population outgrew the resources. From that time onwards, the most appropriate name might well have been the

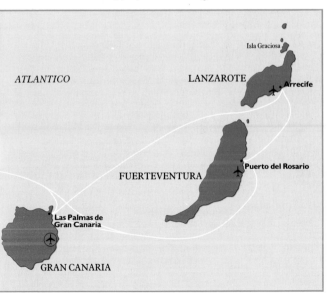

BACKGROUND

Gran Canaria is famous for its beaches, but in the north it has high green hills like these, near Agaete

Unfortunate Islands. Grinding poverty led to mass emigration, mainly to Latin America. The period of the Civil War and Franco dictatorship – 1936–75 – was harder still for the islands, largely because of neglect from Madrid. Now tourism has brightened prospects immeasurably and the new democratic government of Spain has been careful to put the Canary Islands back on the national map.

Yet even now there are problems, not least in tourism. Overbuilding in the resorts of Tenerife and Gran Canaria, and potential overbuilding in Lanzarote, threatens the very market it was intended to serve. Meanwhile the reduction in the cost of long-haul holidays means that winter sun can be found in more exotic destinations at comparable and sometimes lower prices. The long term result may in the end be beneficial for the Canaries. With growing competition for tourists and the changing demands of the market, the quality of the environment becomes a high priority. And in the end that must serve the best interests of the islander as well as the tourist.

Canarian Balconies

These open-sided balconies of Canarian pine are a delightful and distinctive feature of island architecture. They have carved wooden panels up to knee height or a little higher. The panels are surmounted by prettily-turned balusters. Uprights at the corners support tiled roofs over each balcony.

THE WESTERN ISLANDS: TENERIFE, GOMERA, HIERRO AND LA PALMA

TENERIFE

General Information

Size: 794 square miles (2,057 sq km). Approx 26 miles (42km) east to west across the centre, 27½ miles (44km) north to south, but spreading to 50 miles (80km) along its north coast. Highest point: Pico del Teide, Mt Teide, 12,199ft (3,710m). Population: 600,000.

The volcanic cone of Teide, centrepiece of Tenerife and highest mountain in all of Spain and her possessions, soars out of the Atlantic to stand as the great symbol of the Canary Islands. Teide was actually in eruption as the tiny ships of Columbus sailed past in 1492 on their voyage of discovery. Tenerife has been giving a welcome to visitors from northern Europe since the 19th century, when those under doctor's orders or simply in search of winter warmth would sometimes come here instead of to the French Riviera.
Then, as now, the essential factor was the island's climate. The north coast, always temperate but often cloudy, was the original point of attraction, in part because of its magnificent plants and trees and general sense of plenty. This coast retains its popularity, particularly among the older generation, and today it draws in visitors from the whole of Europe. But as in a number of the Canary Islands, the south of Tenerife has a different microclimate from the north, being altogether hotter and drier. Over recent years, this has proved an irresistible attraction to younger visitors. Huge, entirely modern resorts, posing considerable environmental problems, now boom away on a coast that until just recently had little to show for itself other than harsh black rock and a handful of tiny beaches. This is still not exactly sea-swimming country, despite the introduction of some artificial beaches, but blue skies, hotels and apartments, shops,

Los Roques, one of the bizarre features of Tenerife's volcanic national park

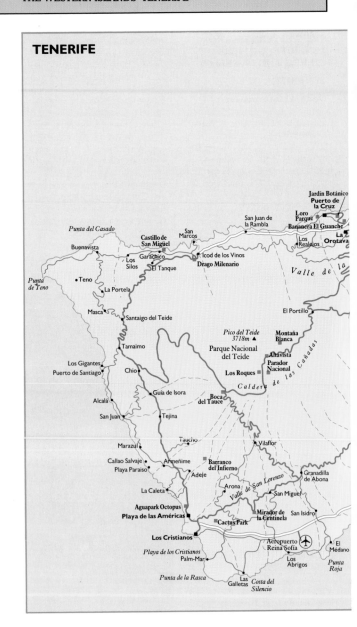

TENERIFE

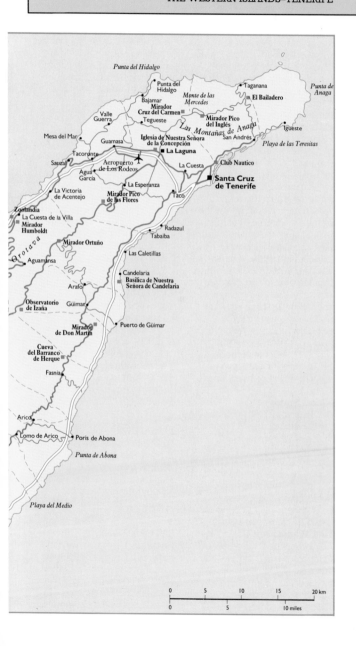

restaurants and discos combine to spread a holiday atmosphere. The other great attraction of Tenerife is the large number of possible excursions to all kinds of entertainments and places of special historic, architectural and scenic interest. In this respect, it is easily the richest of the Canary Islands.

The spectacular volcanic landscape around Teide is a national park: Parque Nacional del Teide. The trade winds make their first contact with the island at the northeast corner, and the higher peaks here are often enveloped in cloud. This rolls on towards the centre of the islands so that the cone of Teide frequently has a ring of cloud around its middle, leaving the land below clear but sometimes in shadow. Meanwhile the mountain, often snow-covered, rises grandly above its cloudy ring. A fair amount of rain falls in the northwest in particular and along the north coast in general.

Island History

The Spanish nobleman Alonso Fernández de Lugo overcame Guanche resistance during bitter fighting from 1494 to 1496, and the local population appears to have been slowly absorbed. The island was attacked several times, always unsuccessfully, by the British, on the last occasion (1797) by Nelson (see Santa Cruz, **What to See**, below). In 1927, when the Canaries were divided into two provinces, the city of Santa Cruz became capital of the province containing all the western islands – La Palma, Hierro and Gomera, as well as Tenerife

itself. In 1936, General Francisco Franco met here with fellow army officers to plan the coup attempt which led to Spain's bitter civil war.

RESORTS

BAJAMAR
This small resort on the northeast coast was more fashionable 10 years ago than now. Backed by dramatic countryside, it is specially popular with Germans – many have settled in the area – and with Tenerifeans in summer. There is a black sand beach.

EL MÉDANO
This – up to now – quiet resort, curiously undisturbed by the proximity of the airport, is small and quite unstylish, but homey in atmosphere and extremely popular with a loyal band of British visitors. Its natural but not over-large beach is the best on the south coast.

LA CALETA
La Caleta and its area, north of Playa de las Américas, is marked by massive individual buildings. This coast holds out little by way of charm or tolerable beaches.

LAS CALETILLAS
Hemmed in by motorway and power station, this desperate corner somehow sells itself as a resort. It is popular with Spanish students and low budget travellers. Once seen, always resistible.

Los Cristianos has a Mediterranean atmosphere, and is part of a popular resort complex

◆
LAS GALLETAS

Entirely different in character from Los Cristianos just along the coast, Las Galletas consists of low-rise developments, running well back from the sea and set among considerable amounts of space, often with fine gardens. Sea swimming is poor but there are plenty of pools to compensate. A Belgian-inspired development named Ten-Bel overshadows the rest. There is a fairly drab little local town and a small harbour.

◆◆◆
LOS CRISTIANOS

Today Los Cristianos has virtually joined itself on to the end of Playa de las Américas to form the largest resort complex on Tenerife, in size second only to the Maspalomas/Playa del Inglés holiday conurbation on Gran Canaria. Most summer visitors are British, with strong competition from Germans and Scandinavians in winter. Visually the town is amazing, with many brand new apartment complexes of large, not to say staggering dimensions. But whatever it looks like, many visitors appreciate the modern facilities. The kernel is a non-descript nucleus of older town clustered around a harbour which offers shelter for yachts and fishing boats and serves as the starting point for ferry and hydrofoil to the neighbouring island of Gomera. The beach is right beside the harbour, virtually part of it, lively but far too small for the needs of the many holidaymakers. Visitors often opt instead for apartment or hotel swimming pools.

THE WESTERN ISLANDS–TENERIFE

The cliffs called Los Gigantes tower over Puerto de Santiago

LOS GIGANTES/PUERTO DE SANTIAGO

This little resort, growing quite fast thanks to rapid development of time- share apartments, is exceptional for just one reason. It offers a close-up view of the cliffs of Los Gigantes, rising vertically out of the water opposite and reaching straight up into the sky. Boats proceeding along the base of this prodigious cliffscape look ridiculously, frighteningly small.

♦♦♦
PUERTO DE LA CRUZ

The oldest and the most attractive in appearance of the major resorts on Tenerife. Though marred by one or two excessively large buildings, Puerto de la Cruz has a special atmosphere because of its old town. (See also Puerto de la Cruz, **What to See**, below.)

There are numerous hotels at either end of the old town. Puerto de la Cruz has no beach to speak of but offers exceptional opportunities for pool and poolside relaxation. Cloudier, cooler and more cosmopolitan than the south, it is generally preferred by the older generation of British visitors, though there are plenty of young people from other places.

♦♦♦
PLAYA DE LAS AMÉRICAS

This exceptionally busy resort, with almost a gold-rush atmosphere, has grown up since the 1970s without any kind of older nucleus. It lies on the flat, consisting of a busy main street of bars, restaurants and shops, pulsing with neon and flowing with scantily dressed holidaymakers. This 'main drag' runs one block back from the shore, while the young town grows inland. At the southwest end of the strip, there is a quieter zone of hotels, and at the north end a mixed zone of hotels and apartment blocks. Almost all the hotels are very large indeed. The shoreline is in places composed of blackish rock, in other parts of artificial sandy beach contained by stone breakwaters. The beaches become exceedingly crowded, with waterskiing, jet-skiing, parascending and the like just offshore. On land, the atmosphere can sometimes cross the border into rowdiness, particularly in the area of the Verónicas, a series of little commercial centres housing mainly bars, Mostly, though, good-hearted liveliness prevails.

SANTA CRUZ DE TENERIFE

The major Spanish port of Santa Cruz became the capital of all the islands in 1723, replacing La Laguna six miles (10km) away. In 1927 it was demoted somewhat, becoming capital simply of the province of Tenerife, which includes all four western islands. The city now alternates with Las Palmas in Gran Canaria, capital of the eastern islands, as seat of the recently appointed government of the Canary Islands.

Santa Cruz occupies an arc of land between the sea and the base of dramatic, forbidding mountains piled up very steep behind. Moving inland from sea to mountain, the various zones of which the town is made are clearly visible. The first consists of extensive port installations, able to handle everything from yachts to ocean-going trawlers to cruise ships and large tankers. Watching the shipping is one of the pleasures of the town. Next comes a promenade, with the Plaza de España, emotional and touristic hub of town, at its southern end. The main shopping streets lead inland from the Plaza de España. The shopping district occupies only a small area, and quickly gives way to a turn-of-century residential district with handsome villas.

WHAT TO SEE IN SANTA CRUZ

FRANCO MONUMENT
At the opposite end of the front from the Plaza de España and its memorial for the Civil War dead, there stands a highly romanticised monument to General Franco, victor in that war and absolute dictator of Spain from 1939 until his death in 1975.

IGLESIA DE NUESTRA SEÑORA DE LA CONCEPCIÓN
Plaza de la Iglesia
This fine 16th-century church, its tower capped by an octagonal belfry, and the cluster of buildings attached to it, are all that remain of the oldest part of the old town of Santa Cruz, destroyed in living memory and much lamented. Within are Lord Nelson's captured battle flag and the cross allegedly carried by the island's 15th-century Spanish conquerors. Closed for redecoration until 1999.

♦
MERCADO DE NUESTRA SEÑORA DE AFRICA
The Market of Our Lady of Africa is a surprisingly small but

purpose-built walled enclosure and basement full of shops and stalls, with a good deal of animation. It is entered via an arched gateway close to the dry watercourse which cuts through the southern side of the town centre.

◆◆

MUSEO ARQUEOLÓGICO

in the Palacio Insular, Plaza de España: entry on Avenida Bravo Murillo, 3rd floor

Less spectacular than that of Las Palmas on Gran Canaria, this Archaeological Museum nevertheless gives a clear idea of the island community displaced by the Spaniards. It contains fairly simple pottery, clothing of skins, spears without barbs and a room with a skeleton at the doorway and a mass of skulls and jawbones packed tight inside each other (the light switches on rather terrifyingly as your foot makes contact with the threshold). Most fascinating of all are the Guanche mummies.

Open: Monday to Saturday 09.00–13.00hrs, 16.00–18.00hrs.
Closed: Sunday.

◆◆

MUSEO MUNICIPAL DE BELLAS ARTES

José Murphy 4

The Fine Arts Museum has ship models, arms and armour, coins – but best are the paintings. The collection includes some Flemish and Spanish masters and more recent Canarian works. The museum is in the Plaza del Principe, an agreeable square with trees and bandstand. Note

in one corner the fine plasterwork and elaborate decoration of the Circulo de Amistad de Enero 1855 (Circle of Friendship of January 1855). Adjoining the square and museum, though facing on to the street below, the church of San Francisco has barley sugar columns and an elegantly

SANTA CRUZ DE TENERIFE

curvaceous top to its façade.
Open: Monday to Friday,
10.00–20.00hrs, winter;
10.00–13.00hrs, summer.
Closed: Saturday, Sunday.

◆◆
PARQUE SANTIAGO GARCÍA SANABRIA

A relaxed and shady park in

the heart of town, with thickets
of bamboo, handsome trees
and exotics. In the centre, a
massive monument with
plenty of unclothed torso pays
tribute to the local worthy after
whom the park is named.
There is a floral clock, too,
much photographed by
visitors.

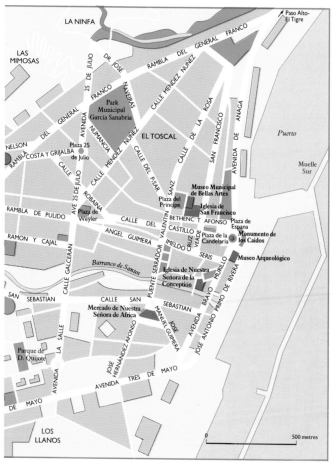

◆
PASO ALTO
Promenade
El Tigre, the cannon which removed Lord Nelson's arm, is on display here at the northern end of the promenade, just past the Club Nautico.

◆◆
PLAZA DE ESPAÑA
This is the hub of Santa Cruz, set on the front between harbour and town. Its main building is the large grey block of the Palacio Insular, seat of the island government. It also houses the tourist information office and archaeological museum (see above). The sombre Palacio Insular looks out on to an equally sombre monument to those who fell in the Spanish Civil War

Civil War monument in the Plaza de España, Santa Cruz

(1936–9). The monument is tall and grey, with a long reflecting mirror set into each side in the shape of a crusader's sword.

◆
PLAZA DE LA CANDELARIA
A pedestrianised rectangle lying just on the town side of the Plaza de España and giving access to the Calle del Castillo (see **Shopping**, below). The seaward side of the square is adorned with an important monument, the late 18th-century Triumph of the Virgin of Candelaria, by the Italian Antonio Canova, celebrating the Spanish conquest of the Guanches. The Virgin is on top of a tall column, with four conquered Guanche chieftains beneath her.

◆
PLAZA 25 DE JULIO
This normally disregarded square, or rather circle, has a fine ceramic pond and set of benches bearing 1920s style advertisements, all done in decorative tiles.

◆◆
LAS TERESITAS
San Andrés, six miles (10km) northwest of Santa Cruz
Las Teresitas is a hoop of golden sand imported from the Sahara. The sand is held firmly in place by a system of breakwaters. It is easily the best stretch of beach on Tenerife, heavily used in summer by townspeople from Santa Cruz and La Laguna, but deserted in winter. Since foreigners are keen to swim at times when good Canarians stay well-wrapped up indoors, there have been many schemes for tourist development of the land

behind Las Teresitas. Debates are acrimonious; the future uncertain.

WHAT TO SEE OUTSIDE SANTA CRUZ

◆◆
ANAGA MOUNTAINS
These are the extremely steep but not very high mountains 3,360ft (1,024m) which back the city of Santa Cruz de Tenerife and form a high backbone to the island's northeast corner. A road from La Laguna (or Tegueste) follows the most dramatic portions of the range, offering a series of fine lookout points, some back over La Laguna, others out over the precipitous countryside and down to the sea below. Taken in order, these viewpoints are Cruz del Carmen, Pico del Inglés and El Bailadero. It is also possible to climb up from San Andres, on the coast north of Santa Cruz, in which case the viewpoints will be reached in reverse order. From El Bailadero, a road descends steeply to remote Taganana. Vegetation is surprisingly lush, with 'laurasilva' or laurel forest at medium altitude. It is often misty in this corner of the island: save the route for a clear day.

CALDERA DE LAS CAÑADAS
See **Parque Nacional del Teide**

◆
CANDELARIA
fifteen miles (24km) southwest of Santa Cruz
The Basilica de Nuestra Señora de Candelaria, sited towards the south of this growing coastal town, is the island's main place of

The church at Candelaria is a place of pilgrimage

pilgrimage. Visitors to the church first enter a huge open square with, to the left along the sea wall, large pseudo-primitive sculptures of Guanche chieftains. A very big, newly built church occupies the far side of the square. Within, and as like as not surrounded by wagon loads of strelitzia, roses and carnations, there stands an unremarkable but richly dressed statue of the Virgin. According to legend, a statue of the Virgin was miraculously washed ashore here during the days of the pagan Guanches, and its presence made Candelaria a shrine for the Spaniards when they later arrived.

The 3,000-year-old dragon tree at Icod de los Vinos

ICOD DE LOS VINOS

Signs point you to the 'Millenary Dragon', the 3,000-year-old dragon tree which makes this small town almost a compulsory stopping-place. And yes, the tree is fantastic, dwarfing the tour buses which cluster around. Its monstrous trunk is hour-glass shaped, looking as if composed of concrete rivulets (with a little real concrete about its base). An unbelievable number of twisty branches spring out from the top of the trunk and at the end of each is what looks like a fiercely primitive cactus. To one side, above the dragon tree and round an attractive old church, a great number of lesser but still spectacular trees of many species stand on a large terrace. Above is a little square where the pleasant old buildings have time-worn Canarian balconies.

GARACHICO

This little coastal town offered the best harbour on the north coast up to 1706 when it was rudely filled in by a tide of lava from an eruption above. Several historic buildings survived and together with the rebuilt (but already antique) streets they make this one of the prettiest places in Tenerife, with plenty of wooden Canarian balconies. There is a harbour, too, though more modest than the original. The high hills behind are so steep as to be almost cliffs. Just offshore is the Roque de Garachico, a large black rock, almost an islet.

LA LAGUNA

Alonso Fernandez de Lugo, conqueror of Tenerife, established La Laguna as his capital in 1496. On the high neck of the northeast promontory and set beside a lake which has since dried out, it has tended recently to spill in all directions. But the old centre remains one of the most pleasant places in Tenerife. It has an air of faded dignity, with impressive portals and façades, one outstanding church and a selection of old streets and squares which are a delight to wander in.

Calle de San Agustin

Perhaps the most interesting single street in La Laguna, it leads from the general area of the Concepción church (see below) past the grey stone belfry of the Instituto Cabrera Pinto, the Convent of San Agustin, the baroque Episcopal Palace and the sterner façade of the old university building, before bringing you, after a walk of perhaps 10 minutes, to the vicinity of the Plaza del Adelantado (see below).

Cathedral

Pink,white and grey,complete with modest dome,the cathedral has a duck pond, lively with Muscovies, right by its main front. The building, founded in the early 16th century, achieved its current form at the start of the present century.

Iglesia de Nuestra Señora de la Concepción

One of the finest church buildings on Tenerife, long, low and cream coloured with stone trimmings, and dominated by a handsome tower. Within, note the dark and elaborately carved pulpit and statue of the Virgin, her left breast pierced by a most realistic-looking, shiny sword.

Plaza del Adelantado

A square with handsome buildings and a real sense of Old Spain. On the corner of the square and the narrow cranny of the Calle Dean Palahl, the convent of Santa Catalina has a notable Canarian balcony (in this case, a gallery) with elaborate wooden lattice work.

◆◆
MASCA

Teno, northwest Tenerife
At the heart of the mountainous Teno district, Masca is a must for lovers of dramatic scenery. The

narrow road from Tamaimo first climbs up over a small ridge offering notable views of Teide behind and above. Once across the ridge, it descends steeply through tight hairpins, revealing a countryside deeply cleft by ravines. Sharp ridges rise like the backs of dinosaurs to the height of the road. The ancient roofs of the much-visited village lie beneath the road. Looking back, one sees that the ravine positively bristles with rocky outcrops, and glistens with wind-blown palms. The road continues, high and thrilling but generally well guarded, to La Portela. It then follows an easy descent to Buenavista on the north coast. (This journey is equally dramatic the other way round.)

◆◆◆
LA OROTAVA ✓

Valle de la Orotava
Though not very far above Puerto de la Cruz, this town has a firmly defined character of its own. Its old centre, still remarkably well preserved, houses a rich jumble of mansions, convent and monastery, pleasing public places and substantial churches.

Casa de los Balcones

This mansion on the Calle de San Francisco has been converted into a museum/shop of local handicrafts, and makes a convenient starting point for exploring the town. It lives up to its name, which means 'House of Balconies'. Those outside are really galleries rather than balconies, rather too obviously

Near La Orotava: a traditional-style balcony overlooks the garden

conserved. Inside, two tiers of beautiful and elaborate balconies rise above a pretty, ancient-feeling courtyard. Just opposite is another noteworthy mansion used for the same purposes – La Casa del Turista, dating from 1590.

Hijuela del Botánico
The name literally means 'Little Daughter of the Botanic Garden' – the one in Puerto de la Cruz. It is a densely packed garden of trees and shrubs behind the town hall, with a dragon tree at the centre.

Hospital of the Holy Trinity
near the Casa de los Balcones
A doorway immediately below the main building gives on to a terrace/balcony offering a view of the beautiful but increasingly built-up Valle de la Orotava. Set into the main door of the hospital, also on the terrace, is a revolving wooden drum, open on one side. According to the tale, unwanted babies were deposited in the open side of the barrel. One twirl and off they went through the door to care and safety within.

Iglesia de Nuestra Señora de la Concepción
A late 18th-century church. To the left of the large alabaster altar (a survival from an earlier church on the same spot) there is a large screen of the Conception, to the right a grey-painted screen apparently carved from stone. Tap it and you will see that it is wooden. Masses of flowers usually adorn this baroque building, centre of the Corpus Christi flower festival.

Plaza de la Constitución
Yellow cassias bloom in ordered

rows around a cream-coloured bandstand in this delectable spot with its fine views towards the coast. At one extreme stands the yellow façade of San Agustín, with Canarian carved doors. From further along the square, a steep garden, rich in strelitzias and flowering shrubs, ascends towards the ornate building of the **Liceo de Taoro**. This is a private club where members doze on plum-coloured sofas in a kind of Victorian time-warp. Exhibitions and recitals are held here; the public is admitted.

♦♦♦

PARQUE NACIONAL DEL TEIDE ✓

Mount Teide, huge and impressive as it is, was not the original centre or high-point of the island. This was a yet greater volcanic mountain standing immediately to the south. Millions of years ago, the ancient monster either erupted or collapsed in on itself, leaving a gigantic crater. Mount Teide is no more than a large cone lying on the edge of this crater, which in its way is even more spectacular than Teide itself. The name of the crater is Caldera de las Cañadas. The crater and Mount Teide together make up the Teide National Park.

Getting there
The journey up from the coast is part of the event, and is quite different on either side of the mountain. The climb from the comparatively arid south – via San Isidro, Granadilla and Vilaflor or from Playa de las Américas via Chio – starts in scrubby, ravine-rent country, passes through vineyards and finally sparse pine forest before bringing the visitor over the lip of the crater and down into its awesomely rocky bowl. The Granadilla/Vilaflor road enters via a striking pass, the **Boca de Tauce**. The journey from the north – directly up from Puerto de la Cruz and La Orotava or along the northeast ridge from La Laguna and La Esperanza – leads through well-cultivated farmland, with flowers and patches of sweet corn, then up through often cloudy, moist green forest, and so across the lip into the crater. Even if Mount Teide appears from below to be blocked off by cloud, the chances are that all will be clear on top.

Caldera de las Cañadas
The crater lies at about 6,200ft (2,000m). It is 30 miles (48km) in circumference and 10 miles (16km) in diameter, with Teide rising above to the north and the remainder enclosed by high rock walls. In places these rise over 1,550ft (500m) from the floor of the crater. Sometimes black, sometimes red, this is mostly a wild mass of bare volcanic stone. It lies in huge ridges as if shoved into untidy form by bulldozers. A rib of extravagantly-shaped rocks – **Los Roques** – at one point runs across the floor of the crater from Teide towards the outer rim. Near the Boca de Tauce a mirador (lookout point) leads the eye upwards towards a pair of blackened holes on a lesser mountainside – **las Narices**, the Nostrils, scene of the island's most recent eruption, at the end of the 18th century.

Teide

This loftiest of Spanish mountains, with views over the whole chain of the Canary Islands, has attracted visitors for hundreds of years, among them the German botanist Alexander von Humboldt and the astronomer Jean Mascourt. In 1910, Mascourt took the first photographs of Halley's comet from the mountain. The ascent on foot traditionally took two days, starting from La Orotava and with a stop at Altavista, site of the present mountain refuge. Today most visitors go up by cable car. This climbs, in eight minutes from 7,730ft (2,356m) to 11,670ft (3,555m), leaving a further 524ft (160m) to climb on foot in the thin air. The cable car carries 33 people at a time and from mid-morning long queues wait below.

Departures: 09.00–16.00 hrs, return until 19.00 hrs.

National Park Information

On entry to the park in the northwest, at **El Portillo** (close to the junction of the roads from La Orotava and La Laguna) there is a visitors' centre offering information on guided and/or signposted walks and more ambitious hikes. (Some information can also be obtained in tourist information offices.)

◆◆
PUERTO DE LA CRUZ

The attractive old town of Puerto de la Cruz is clustered round the former harbour, or *puerto* and a lively square, Plaza del Charco. All the town's historic sights are in this area, with other interesting spots to visit within a couple of miles (3-4km).

Caldera de Las Cañadas, the crater of a once-huge volcano

Avenida de Colón

A promenade on the northeast side of the town, where the sea-walls provide often-spectacular displays of breaking surf. The Avenida de Colón (Columbus) adjoins the Lido Martiánez (see below) and under the general heading 'Costa Martiánez/Café Columbus' is the starting point of many free bus services to local entertainments.

Bananera El Guanche

Just over a mile (2km) from town,

on past the Botanical Garden on the road to La Orotava, the Bananera explains all about the banana. It shows an informative video every 20 minutes and offers a chance to wander in a working banana plantation. Free glass of liqueur. Free bus from Costa Martiánez/Café Columbus.

Capilla de San Telmo
A simple but very pleasing whitewashed chapel on the front, with a florally painted, Canarian-style altar screen.

Casino Taoro
This large and rather stately ex-hotel above the town, floodlit at night, plies its business as a casino every day of the year. Visitors must be over 18 and carry passports. Free taxi from town, entrance fee.

Iglesia de la Peña de Francia
From its panelled wooden ceiling, with beams cutting across the space below, to the ceramic plaques on the walls and its setting in a pleasant tree-lined square, the principal church of Puerto de la Cruz is pure Canarian in feeling. Sculptures by Luján Pérez, local 18th-century culture hero.

Jardín Botánico/Jardín de Aclimatación

on the main road into Puerto de la Cruz, La Paz district
The founder and first director of the Botanical/Acclimatisation Garden was the aptly named Marques de Villanueva del Prado (1788–1832, Prado meaning meadow). The aim was to acclimatise plants and trees to the Canarian climate, then move them on to the Spanish mainland. The plants and trees (as also orchids in the orchid house) have done almost excessively well, though few have made the final transfer to Spain. The garden is currently being extended and replanted.

Lido Martiánez

The answer to the beachlessness of Puerto de la Cruz has been provided by noted Lanzarote architect César Manrique. An ample site on the sea front, effectively a promontory backed by the earliest cluster of tourist hotels, has been dramatically fashioned into an area of pools and poolside pleasure. White walls top black volcanic rock, palms nod over light blue lagoons, a large and lumpy rock suddenly reveals itself as the most profuse of fountains while all around, outside, the Atlantic swells and surges. A moderate daily charge gives access to all facilities.

Loro Parque

on the western side of town, just over a mile (2km) from the centre
This aviary set in a park contains the world's largest collection of parrots. The birds are paired off in large cages, with displays illustrating the continents where

Some of the colourful inhabitants of the Loro Parque

they originated. The well-kept gardens, including a fine show of orchids, are also a pleasure. Sea lions, sharks and dolphins as well as the newly developed Punta Brava beach in front of the park make this a popular tourist stop. A substantial breeding programme helps to conserve rare species. Free buses every 20 minutes from the Costa Martiánez in Puerto de la Cruz. *Open:* daily 08.30 to 18.00 hrs.

TEIDE
See **Parque Nacional del Teide**

◆◆
VALLE DE LA OROTAVA
This so-called valley is more of a sloping rift, a wide but steep-walled depression running down from underneath Mount Teide to the sea. There are marvellous views over the 'valley', Puerto de la Cruz and the north coast behind it, from the village of Cuesta de la Villa, the Mirador Humboldt (named after the 19th-century German naturalist) and the town of La Orotava (see separate entry). Considerable recent building, mainly of private houses, has altered the view, but the walking remains good. Maps of footpaths available at tourist information offices.

◆
VALLE GUERRA: CASA DE CARTA
shortly before Valle Guerra (leave Santa Cruz–Puerto de la Cruz motorway at Tacoronte or Guamasa)
The Casa de Carta is an example of old-fashioned Canarian country architecture. It has been turned into the island's official Ethnographical Museum, partnering the Archaeological Museum in Santa Cruz. Exhibits include weaving and needlework, traditional costumes and gofio-making (*gofio* is a kind of all-purpose flour of the islands).
Open: 10.00–13.00hrs, 16.00–19.00 hrs (summer), 15.00–18.00 hrs (winter).
Closed: Friday.

Accommodation
Los Gigantes/Puerto de Santiago
Hotel Santiago, 4 star (tel: 86 72 75), on rocky, built-up promontory, offers spectacular views of Los Gigantes cliffs. Pleasant atmosphere, good food and rooms.

Playa de las Américas
Bitácora Apartment/Hotel, 4 star (tel: 79 15 40), heated swimming pool. **Gran Tinerfe**, 4 star (tel: 79 12 00), good views and position.
Vulcano, 4 star (tel: 79 20 35), impressive balconied court, full of palms and dripping greenery from aloft. Pool. Special rooms and facilities for disabled guests.

Puerto de la Cruz
Meliá Botánico, Richard J. Yeoward s-n, 5 star (tel: 38 14 00). Pleasant tropical gardens, quiet and comfortable.

Santa Cruz
Mencey Hotel José Naveiras 38, 5 star (tel: 27 67 00). This spacious hotel, with gleaming marble floors and huge romantic paintings, is built round patios with Canarian balconies. Lawns and swimming pool. *The* place for business executives on expense accounts.

THE WESTERN ISLANDS–TENERIFE

Children
Playa de las Américas area
The **Aquapark Octopus** has outdoor water-slides and many other diversions, and is one of the most popular entertainments of Tenerife. Free bus from Playa de las Américas and Los Cristianos.
Open: daily, 10.00–18.00 hrs.
The **Cactus Park**, off the motorway between Los Cristianos and the Reina Sofia airport at Desierto Feliz, claims the 'largest cactus collection in the world'. Free bus from various hotels in Playa de las Américas, and in Los Cristianos from Edificio Cristianos 1.
Open: daily, 10.00 to 18.00 hrs.

Puerto de la Cruz area
El Castillo Park and Museum, near Los Realetjos, is a fun spot, with camel rides. Free bus from Costa Martiánez/Café Columbus in Puerto de la Cruz. **Zoolandia** has lions, tigers, llamas and zebras, and describes itself as a 'reserve for Canarian fauna and flora'! Three miles (5km) from Puerto de la Cruz on motorway towards Santa Cruz near La Orotava. Free bus from Costa Martiánez. Refer to Puerto de la Cruz for **Loro Parque**, a wonderful parrot aviary with other entertainments, and **Bananera el Guanche**.

Culture, Entertainment and Nightlife
Exhibitions, concerts and so on tend to flourish most vigorously in the north, particularly in **Santa Cruz**, **Puerto de la Cruz** and **La Laguna**. Rock concerts are sometimes held at the former bullring in Santa Cruz. Nightclubs and discos are plentiful. In Puerto de la Cruz, **Andromeda**, underneath the Lido Martiánez, puts on Spanish and international shows. The **Victoria**, by the Tenerife Playa Hotel, is a popular disco and, like **El Coto** at the Hotel Botanico, good but not cheap. In Playa de las Americas, **Melody's**, under the Hotel Ponderosa, attracts the over 25's. **Dry Martini**, by the Guayarmina Princess Hotel, is a first floor restaurant with an excellent jazz bar downstairs. Sophisticates also head for **Bugatti**, below the Royal Garden Apartments, to hear music till dawn. For disco pubs, choice is wider than variety.

Restaurants
Look out for roadside stalls, particularly on the north coast. These may sell local wines, chestnuts roasted in ashes, and hot, salt sardines.

Adeje
The one and only restaurant in Adeje, up above Playa de las Américas, serves chicken marinated in mojo sauce and then deep fried, in taste halfway between Delhi and Kentucky.

Agua García
This village draws large crowds of Tenerifeans for Sunday lunch, the sure test of local quality. (Leave the Santa Cruz/Puerto de la Cruz motorway at Tacoronte and travel a short distance inland). Try **El Junquito** or **El Bosque** (simple and hearty, with meat, salad and wine) or **La Florida**, specialising in pork.

La Cuesta de la Villa
High marks for two restaurants neighbouring one another in La

Cuesta de la Villa, a village with fine views over Puerto de la Cruz and the Orotava valley. **El Lagar** (tel: 30 08 75) is good quality international, **Los Corales** (tel: 30 02 49) an elegant fish restaurant. Both are expensive.

Garachico
The **Isla Baja** restaurant surrounds the courtyard of an old house opposite the castle, and specialises in fish. Dining room first floor; downstairs is a lively model of the 1706 eruption.

Los Abrigos
The semi-circular front of this village on a rocky bay not far from Reina Sofia airport is composed almost entirely of fish restaurants. It has a cheerful and lively atmosphere, and is unquestionably the fish-dish centre of the south.

Playa de las Américas
At the top end of the scale, try the **Restaurante Casa Vasca**, situated in the patio of the Compostela Beach Hotel, where the Basque landlord/chef offers Basque dishes. The **Banana Garden**, behind the main beach and beside the Palm Beach complex, serves good Mexican and international food. Banana trees and parrots provide colour. There is live music nightly and flamenco shows at weekends. **Bornajo**, on the main street, is middle range; queues form for tasty grills. **El Gomero**, near the edge of town and owned by a Gomeran, offers cheap, hearty food. Other restaurants worth trying abound in the resort.

Carnations for sale in the flower market, Santa Cruz

Puerto de la Cruz
The **Casa Miranda**, a Canarian mansion on the front near the town hall, is named after its former owners, a Tenerife family whose descendants played a part in the liberation of Latin America. The old mansion is well restored and the dining room is delightful. On the expensive side. Take a five-minute taxi ride out of town in the direction of the Botanical Gardens to **Casa Lala** for cheaper but no less delicious Canarian food. Fish and steaks feature strongly on a small but excellent menu. **Los Gemelos**, just behind the Plaza Charco in the old town, is well recommended for good local cooking and a pleasant atmosphere.

Shopping

Santa Cruz is Tenerife's top shopping centre, despite the arrival of high quality, expensive furs in Puerto de la Cruz and the multitudinous perfume and liquor stores of Playa de las Américas. Most tour companies offer special excursions to Santa Cruz from the resorts, allowing visitors to browse among the Indian-style and often Indian-owned bazaars selling mainly electronic goods. There are some notable handicraft establishments and jewellers. The main shopping area is round the **Plaza de la Candelaria,** including the Calle Castillo (running up from the Plaza de la Candelaria), and Bethencourt Alfonso, running parallel two streets to the northeast. For electronic goods, videos, cameras etc, the main emporium is **Maya**, in a side street off the Plaza de la Candelaria. Good and patient service, no bargaining (as distinct from other bazaar-type shops). Leading handicraft establishments are the excellent **Artespaña**, top right hand corner of Candelaria, and, rather less selective in its stock, the **Casa de los Balcones** on left at entrance to the square from Plaza de España. For **pearls**, try **El Templo** in Bethencourt Alfonso. There are good boutiques in the **Calle Viera y Clavijo** and in the **Rambla de General Franco** near the Hotel Mencey. Cheap **leather goods** are sold near the **Mercado de Nuestra Señora de Africa** and on Sunday mornings there is a *rastro* or **flea market** running along the harbour front from the Club Nautico.

In **Garachico**, **local lace** is on sale in the castle, together with **handicraft items** made by foreign residents. There is a handicraft market here on the first Sunday of each month. **La Orotava** has two busy centres for the sale of Canarian handicrafts – **La Casa de los Balcones** and **La Casa del Turista** opposite, both in the Calle San Francisco.

Special Events

Locals claim that the **Santa Cruz Carnival** (February/March) is second only to that of Rio de Janeiro (they make the same claim in Las Palmas, though). Certainly there is lots of fun and little sleep. For **Corpus Christi** (June) **La Orotava** goes wild with flowers. Carpets of petals and intricate patterns in multi-coloured sand offer a brief, extravagant brilliance. There are many smaller scale local festivals throughout the island, at almost all times of year.

Sport

Already developing quickly on Tenerife, **golf** seems likely to become a major attraction for the future, just as it is in Gran Canaria. The main courses are the Real Golf Club de Tenerife at La Laguna, the Amaralla Golf and Country Club and Golf del Sur (both Playa de las Américas area).

In the same area there is **go-karting** at the Karting Club Tenerife and at Karting Las Américas (free bus to the latter from Playa de las Américas). Real Club Náutico, Santa Cruz de Tenerife, is for **yachts** and **motorboating**, with other facilities such as **tennis**.

GOMERA

General Information
Size: 146 square miles (378 sq km). 14½ miles (23km) north to south and 15½ miles (25km) east to west.
Highest point: 4,878ft (1,487m).
Population: 20,000.

Though only 35 minutes by hydrofoil from Tenerife, Gomera is thoroughly unspoiled. It is extraordinarily high in relation to its small land surface, ranking almost with La Palma in this respect; and it is notable for the 'laurasilva' or laurel forest covering its upper surfaces. The Gomerans are a frank and friendly people, inhabiting one of the most splendidly beautiful of the Canary Islands.

In shape, Gomera is like a very tall cake from which alternate slices have been cut, sometimes slightly off centre. These missing slices are thrillingly deep ravines; to get from one place to another, you are always wiggling up from sea level and over the centre of the island, then descending into another of the ravines. On top of the cake and in places running down the sides, Gomera has its icing of laurasilva forests. The collision of trade winds and the Gomera mountains produces mist and cloud, drizzle and downpour on the heights, and it is this which makes the forest grow so abundantly. Most of the high centre is a national park – the Parque Nacional de Garajonay. Around the base of the island, more often than not, the sun shines brilliantly – on comparatively infertile, stony

A typical contrast of wild cacti and farmland in the spectacular Valle Gran Rey

ground in the south, and on vines, bananas, palms, tomatoes and tropical fruit in the valleys of the north.

The other extraordinary feature of the island is *el silbo*, the whistling language invented for communicating across the ravines. Immensely powerful sounds are achieved, either by whistling through the fingers or by simple force of lip and air. The sound of the whistle is used in part as a substitute for vocalisation – when you hear it, you almost think you can understand – and partly in ways which are quite impenetrable. It is hard to learn and though some older people still know the 'language', the younger generation frequently understands but cannot 'speak', or rather whistle.

Island History

Gomera is famous chiefly because this was Columbus's final port of call – the last place his foot touched ground – before the historic journey of 1492. He returned again in 1493 and in 1498, on both occasions using Gomera as a stepping stone for further journeys to the Americas. The island had first been visited on behalf of Spain at the start of the 15th century, by the Norman Jean de Béthencourt, well remembered throughout the Canaries in street names. Hernán Peraza the Elder finally conquered it for Spain in the middle of the century. The tyrannical younger Peraza was murdered by his subjects, leaving his widow, the beautiful and formidable Beatriz de Bobadilla, in control.

GOMERA

Punta del Peligro
Los Organos
Playa de Vallehermoso
Punta de Agulo
Vállehermoso
Agulo
Las Rosas
Punta Gabiña
Alojera
El Roque Cano
Macayo
Hermigua
Taguluche
Arure
El Cedro
Punta Majona
Parque Nacional de Garajonay
Valle de Hermigua
El Cercado
Garajonay 1487m
La Zarzita
Bosque del Cedro
La Calera
Chipude
La Fortaleza
Roques de Agando
Parador Conde de Gomera
Valle Gran Rey
Igualero
Benchijigua
Vagaipala
San Sebastián de la Gomera
Vueltas
Alajeró
Punta Gorda
La Rajita
Antoncojo
Playa de Santiago
Punta Falcones
Punta del Becerro

0 2 4 6 km
0 2 4 miles

The island remained in the possession of the Counts of Gomera until the 19th century. Its harbour was frequently visited by vessels crossing the Atlantic, and it became as closely involved with the New World as the Old. Economic distress forced many of its inhabitants to emigrate to Latin America. The island suffered particularly under the Franco dictatorship, a time remembered with bitterness. Even today, many Gomerans emigrate, most often now to work in tourism on neighbouring Tenerife.

There are no resorts at all in the sense in which the word applies in Tenerife and Las Palmas, but there is a notable parador and one large hotel complex.

SAN SEBASTIÁN DE LA GOMERA

The island's miniature capital lies behind the bay which Columbus and other early navigators used as an anchorage. Today it is a regular little port, with a quay on the outer side, and a stony beach in front of the town. The ferry leaves three times a day (twice on Tuesdays) for Los Cristianos on Tenerife; two hydrofoils make faster and more frequent crossings. Work on the construction of an airport has begun but no one expects it to be completed before 2000. Within moments of landing, travellers find themselves in a little tree-filled square (or circle) – the Plaza de América – behind the front. All the town's monuments lie within a few minutes' walk, not to mention the baker, the town hall and island buses.

WHAT TO SEE IN SAN SEBASTIÁN

CASA COLUMBINA
Calle del Medio
Calle del Medio is a little street running inland from the market. Columbus is said to have stayed in this house, and it is at any rate agreeably ancient. Exhibitions concerning La Gomera and its history are put on here. The house is the focus of annual Columbus celebrations in September.

IGLESIA DE LA ASUNCIÓN
Calle del Medio
Some parts of the church may have been in existence when Columbus said his prayers here in 1492 but the bulk of it is 16th century. On entering, it is well worth turning to look back at the handsome dark wood balcony above the doorway. To the left of the (wooden) altar is the Capilla del Pilar, the Chapel of the Pillar, built to commemorate the repulse of an English fleet under Admiral Charles Windham in 1743. A mural, whose lower portions are now lost, shows cannon balls whizzing about. The Puerta del Perdón – Door of Forgiveness – was used by Beatriz de Bobadilla to trick the murderers of her husband. She promised pardon to those who passed through it, thus acknowledging their guilt. And then she executed them.

POZO DE COLÓN
The name means Columbus's Well. Just by the vast tree in the market square there stands a

chunkily stone-built, tightly shuttered, single storey house with patio – the former Customs House, now in the private occupation of a caretaker family. In the centre of the humble patio, a little low well edged with pebbles is honoured as the spot from which Columbus's ships drew water before departing on 6 September 1492. A sign says in Spanish, 'The water from this well baptised America'.

TORRE DEL CONDE

The 'Count's Tower' is a small but stout fort just behind the front. Built in 1447 by Hernán Peraza the Elder, it is the town's most obvious monument. Beatriz de Bobadilla used it as a refuge after the slaying of her husband, Hernán Peraza the Younger, in 1487, and it is here that the popular imagination brings her together with Columbus. Surrounded as it is these days by a car park, with just the odd palm tree for relief, it looks a little melancholy.

WHAT TO SEE OUTSIDE SAN SEBASTIÁN

AGULO

Perched above the sea with views of Tenerife and Teide, and backed by an amphitheatre of rock, this is a quiet, settled village with cobbled streets. Around a church with a strange, domed roof, the Plaza de Leoncio Bento is a pretty place of pollarded trees and houses with wide wooden doorways. Corniche driving in this part of the island surpasses the French Riviera for beauty.

♦
ALOJERA

Far below the main road, but still at some height above the sea, this scattered village occupies an up-and-down patch of land. Below again, after a very steep final descent, there is a modest grey beach where amenities seem likely to expand. The way down from main road to village is unusual: it runs on the outside of the hill rather than inside a ravine. The effect is dramatic.

♦
EL CERCADO

Pottery is produced in this village without benefit of anything so new-fangled as the potter's wheel. Shaped by hand, dabbed in a shiny liquid clay and brushed to take the shine off, it is fired in simple kilns that look like stone-built dog-kennels. The brushwood for the fire is fetched, on foot, from the forest above; the clay is fetched, on foot, from two ravines away. The resulting dishes and jugs look very similar to Guanche pottery on display in the museums of Las Palmas and Santa Cruz de Tenerife.

GARAJONAY
See **Parque Nacional de Garajonay**

HERMIGUA

A steep descent through a beautiful and fertile valley, where vines grow on bamboo lattices, leads down to several little clusters of village running down a ridge. This is the largest centre of habitation after San Sebastián and a sign, in Spanish, welcomes visitors to what it claims is 'the best climate in the world'.

Time seems to have stood still in El Cercado, where pottery is made by traditional methods

Poinsettias blaze obligingly, dates on palm trees gleam bright orange, huge bunches of bananas may be almost emerald and where women carry buckets on their heads.

◆◆
LA FORTALEZA
This is a vast rock outcrop to the southwest of the peak of Garajonay, believed to have been held sacred by the Guanches. There are fine views from several lookout points, among them the Mirador of Igualero on the way down to Playa de Santiago.

◆◆
LOS ORGANOS
One of the marvels of the island. Not far from the Playa de Vallehermoso but visible only from the sea, the rocky northwest coast provides an

unusual display – a great rock organ composed of thousands of pipes or flutes of basalt packed together as if intentionally. Boat trips from Valle Gran Rey, Playa de Santiago and elsewhere.

◆◆◆
PARQUE NACIONAL DE GARAJONAY

Whether visitors plan to walk the paths and mountain trails of Gomera or merely to drive the upland roads, the Garajonay national park, covering most of the high interior, will inevitably be one of the main attractions on the island. Its borders follow, fairly exactly, the limits of the ancient 'laurasilva' laurel forests. The dense evergreens of the forest, the spectacular and deeply rent countryside and the tall, eroded rockstacks of Agando, Ojila, Zarcita and Cherelepin help to make time spent in the park memorable. The forest of El Cedro is also specially recommended.

Founded in 1981, the park was declared a World Heritage Site in 1986. There is an information centre at Juego de Bolas (the Game of Bowls) near Las Rosas on the northern side of the island. This provides details of flora and fauna, waymarked trails and other information.

VALLE GRAN REY

Wild, steep and narrow at the top, a cleft of valley opens beneath the upland village of Arure, offering dramatic viewing points. Two branches of this valley soon run together and broaden downwards into a single rent in the structure of the island. Terraces climb astonishingly

Every possible bit of land is used for farming in the Valle Gran Rey

high on either side with groups of houses clustered like swallows' nests. The valley floor is green and fertile, rich in palms and bananas. The main village lies just near the sea, climbing a little upwards. Right down on the coast, to left, there is a harbour and, to right, a beach. Both have settlements behind and both are in the process of slow and shambolic tourist development, despite local protest. The sandy beach offers the best sea swimming on an island which is generally disappointing in this respect.

VALLEHERMOSO

Remarkable mainly for featuring in vistas from high above in the Garajonay national park, Vallehermoso lies underneath El Roque Cano, the Dog Rock, a tremendous stump stripped bare by erosion and looking much like a canine tooth. At the Playa de Vallehermoso, the mouth of the ravine is strikingly enclosed in rock, with remnants of old port installations. The near-beach of rocks and pebbles can be extremely inhospitable when seas of any size are running.

Accommodation

Part of the charm of Gomera is its comparative lack of accommodation. Apartments and private rooms are to be found in Valle Gran Rey, there are apartments and a handful of 1- and 2-star hotels in San Sebastián, and that is about it, with two striking exceptions. **The Parador Conde de Gomera**, 4 star (tel: 87 11 00), in San Sebastián, is built high on a bluff of cliff above the town, looking

out over the sea and across the straits to Tenerife. Cleverly constructed round patios, purpose-built but agreeably old world, this is by far the most attractive parador in the Canaries and must rank as one of the better small paradors in Spain.
The Hotel Tecina, Lomada de Tecina, 4-star (tel: 89 50 50/89 51 00), at Playa de Santiago, is constructed on the corner of a cliff above the village. Large numbers of two-storey 'bungalows', one room upstairs and one room down, each reached from winding pathways at front-level, stand in luxuriously flowering gardens.

Restaurants
Hermigua
Just between Hermigua and Agulo, the modest **El Silbo** restaurant offers drinks, meals and a terrace with magnificent views.

Parque Nacional de Garajonay
La Laguna Verde, a rough rock building set in a grassy clearing, offers simple, tasty meals. Used by hikers with rucksacks and wet weather gear. Hard to miss.

Playa de Santiago
There are several fish restaurants here. The **Junonia**, and **La Quevita**, both near the port, win top ratings from regulars. They are small and friendly family-run establishments, cheap and appetising. The à la carte restaurant of the **Hotel Tecina**, situated on the beach, is one of the island's two top spots for a serious, expensive meal.

San Sebastián
The restaurant of the parador is the other.

The church in Vallehermoso nestles in sub-tropical greenery

Special Events
Columbus Festival, 6 September.

Sport
The **Hotel Tecina**, Playa de Santiago, has a **gymnasium** and also offers **swimming**, **tennis**, **squash** and **fives** (**frontón**, the Spanish version). There is also tennis and a swimming pool at the **Club Náutico** in San Sebastián (through the tunnel by the quay). But without a doubt the main sport presented by the island is **walking**, more or less strenuously and involving some scrambling, according to the route chosen. Walkers can take themselves along national park trails, and there are Swiss-led hikes for small groups from the Hotel Tecina.

HIERRO

General Information

Size: 107 square miles (278 sq km). 15 miles (24km) from north to south and 17 miles (27km) from east to west.
Highest point: Mount Malpaso 4,925ft (1501m).
Population: 7,400.

The smallest and most westerly of the Canary Islands, enclosed by high cliffs and with only a few beaches, Hierro, like Gomera, is remarkably untouched by tourism. Its most loyal admirers return again and again for just that reason.
The scenery is as spectacular as any in the Canaries. A high, pine-covered ridge runs east to west, curved in the shape of a boomerang. It is, in fact, one half of the rim of a volcanic crater, with the other half invisible beneath the sea. The inner curve of the boomerang falls steeply on the northern side to form a wide bay or gulf – El Golfo – of the greatest beauty. Its slopes are covered in forests of pine and, above the height of 1,650ft (500m), often shrouded in mist, so that the pine-needles drip with moisture. In an island so short of water, this is an invaluable asset. Descending, the pines give way to laurel, beech and giant heathers, then to a huge variety of succulent plants and, finally, green pastures divided by dry stone walls. To the south a triangular landmass reaches down towards the sea and here the pastures turn into bleak volcanic hillsides. It can be wet and misty in the north and east

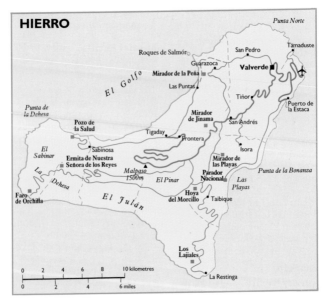

Izique mountain marks the northern end of El Golfo, or 'the gulf', which forms the northern side of boomerang-shaped Hierro

while the sun is shining fit to burst elsewhere on the island. Hierro is a delight for leisurely exploration and best seen on foot. Tarred roads, however, are well maintained and the rough tracks which have to be negotiated are passable by car without too much difficulty.

Island History

Jean de Béthencourt, Norman adventurer and scourge of the Guanches, landed here in 1405 as representative of the Spanish crown. The local king, Armiche, came down from the mountains to greet the visitors. He and his followers, with most of the male population of the island, were immediately enslaved and sent to Europe. One feels that Hierro has never fully recovered. However, the island has one significant claim to fame. Everybody agreed, there was no doubt about it, that the world ended at Hierro, at least until the discovery of America. Up to 1884, when the mantle fell instead to Greenwich in Britain, zero meridian was placed at the island's most westerly point. It was from Hierro that Columbus set off in 1493 on his second journey to America.

Traditionally, most visitors to Hierro are Spaniards, and many come from other Canary Islands. The rest are mainly Germans. There are no resorts as such on Hierro, though there is tourist accommodation at Valverde, Frontera, Tamaduste and La Restinga and, most notably, at the island's parador, out on its own in the bay of Las Playas.

VALVERDE

This very modest town is about four miles (7km) from the airport and about six miles (10km) from Puerto de la Estaca, where the ferry docks. The foundations were laid at the end of the 15th century on the site of an earlier pre-Hispanic settlement. Valverde means Green Valley, a name more accurately applicable to the view from the town.

All the basic necessities may be found in its two main streets: essential shops, banks, the tourist office, a hotel, some bars, a petrol station. But it is the sort of place where you can stand in the dead centre and hear only cocks crowing. There are, though, some interesting sights to see.

WHAT TO SEE IN VALVERDE

◆

IGLESIA DE LA CONCEPCIÓN

This substantial parish church in the main square was built in the late 18th century on the site of an earlier 16th-century one. In stern grey stone and brilliant white, the broad, triple-aisled front rises to a small tower with a lookout balcony. This is one of many Canarian churches used as a refuge against pirate attack.

◆

MUSEO INSULAR

Calle Dr Quintero 11
Situated above the island's tourist office, the Folk Museum exhibits old domestic implements and tools, and local folk costume. It is currently closed for refurbishment and no one dares hazard a guess as to when it will re-open.

◆

MUSEO JUAN PEDRÓN

Calle Previsor Magdalena 8
A private house in old Canarian style with a collection of local antiquities. The house and patio are as interesting as the exhibits. Bang on the door and someone may let you in.

WHAT TO SEE OUTSIDE VALVERDE

◆◆◆
EL PINAR ✓

These forests of Canary pines are the most characteristic feature of Hierro, beautiful to drive through, and even better on foot. In either case you can organise your route to pass various miradors (lookouts) with breathtaking views of the east coast.

The **Mirador de las Playas** offers a view of the wide curve of Las Playas bay with the Roques Bonanza, a strange rock formation rising straight out of the sea a few feet from the shore. On a clear day you can see Gomera, La Palma and Tenerife. Further south there is the **Mirador de Tanajora** and in the forest, **Hoya del Morcillo**, a favourite place for Herreños at weekends who come to picnic (barbecue-fuel provided), play football or go walking. There is also a children's playground, toilets, running water and free camping facilities.

◆◆
EL SABINAR

A wood of juniper trees unique to Hierro (Juniperus sabina). The bark of these bizarrely shaped, wind-twisted trees gives off a pungent aroma and was formerly used as moth repellent. Located a short way down the track north from the Ermita de Nuestra Señora de los Reyes (see separate entry).

◆◆
ERMITA DE NUESTRA SEÑORA DE LOS REYES

This is the Hermitage of Our Lady of the Kings, the patroness of the island, whose shrine is a little white church in the plain of La Dehesa in the west.

A row of whitewashed cabins by the church contains simple cells with bed and cooking facilities for pilgrims.

The story is that on 6 January 1546 ship-wrecked sailors offered the image to local shepherds in exchange for food and water. Carrying the image back home, the shepherds looked down to the coast and saw that the ship had miraculously set sail.

The next miracle followed a lengthy drought. The islanders carried the image of the virgin down to Valverde imploring the Deity for rain, and obtained good results, particularly for an island with an average annual rainfall of only 12 in (300mm). Now every four years (1993, 1997 etc) in commemoration of the miraculous downpour, the image is taken down to Valverde in the first weekends in July, with singing, dancing and festivities.

◆
FARO DE ORCHILLA

The Orchilla Lighthouse, at the opposite end of the island from Valverde, at Punta Orchilla, is still a navigational aid for ships

The Ermita (hermitage) of La Dehesa houses an image which is said to have worked miracles

coming from Latin America. The lighthouse itself cannot be visited but there is a tiny beach of black sand near it. If you manage to get down there the reward is a safe swim off a jetty. Another prize is a certificate issued by the tourist office at Valverde testifying that the bearer has been to 'The end of the World'.

FRONTERA

The fertile nucleus of the fruit and wine growing region of Hierro and administrative centre of the south and west, Frontera is the ideal base for a walking holiday. The free-standing belfry of the village church of Candelaria has been built on a volcanic boulder, and is a local curiosity.

LA RESTINGA

A fishing village on the southern tip of the island, now beginning to attract some tourists. The harbour is protected by an effective but unattractive breakwater, making it possible to swim in calm waters off a small black beach. Clear water off the coast provides good diving, with facilities and tuition available locally. To judge by the amount of new apartment building underway at Restinga, and the bars and restaurants which already exist, this is the nearest thing in Hierro to a tourist resort. The road north from La Restinga goes through old volcanic craters and lava fields, frequented at weekends by rabbit-hunters with dogs and ferrets. In this weird landscape, strands of lava, known as **Los Lajiales**, have cooled and petrified like coils of rope laid out

The harsh northern coast near the Roques de Salmór

on flat rocks. The cooled lava has also formed caves and tunnels winding down for miles to the sea. These are on private land but every lad in the area knows precisely where the tunnels are and feels free to explore them.

MIRADOR DE LA PEÑA

Designed by the Lanzarote architect César Manrique in his own distinctive style, this lookout with cliffs falling away on all sides offers outstanding views of the wide sweep of the bay of El Golfo. The mirador is also a restaurant.

pleasant promenade follows the bay at different levels.
Tamaduste is so close to Valverde airport that you can see the control tower, but the light Fokker aircraft on inter-island routes are a point of interest rather than an irritation.

◆
ROQUES DE SALMÓR
These are two huge rocks rising out of the sea north of the Mirador de la Peña viewpoint. For many years they were the focus of attention as the home of huge primeval lizards indigenous to Hierro and sometimes as long as 40in (1m). Publicity made them prey to dealers and collectors and when it became clear they were in danger of extinction they were removed from the Roques de Salmór. A zoo where they can be safely housed and bred while remaining on view to the public is under construction in the small village of Guinea.

Accommodation

Frontera
With only four double bedrooms, the **Punta Grande Hotel**, Las Puntas, 2 star (tel: 55 90 81) is listed in the Guinness Book of Records as the smallest hotel in the world. What it lacks in size, it makes up for in interest and comfort, sitting as it does on a small fist of land stuck out into a wild sea and with an awesome backdrop of mountains. In former days it was a warehouse. The restaurant serves excellent fresh fish. The village of Frontera, 1,150ft (350m) above the coast has pension and apartments suitable as a base for walking holidays.

◆
POZO DE LA SALUD
two miles (3km) outside the village of Sabinosa.
Complete with sulphur and radium, the Pozo de la Salud ('Well of Health') is the only spring on the island. A spa hotel is currently under construction. Sabinosa itself is a centre of wine production and basket weaving.

◆◆
TAMADUSTE
This is the only village on the island with a seaside holiday feel, due largely to its position round a sheltered little bay. Small boats ride at anchor at high tide and children dive off a board protruding from the jetty. A

Las Playas Bay
The **Parador de la Isla de El Hierro**, 3 star (tel: 55 80 36) is at the foot of a steep cliff, seven miles (12km) south from the Puerto de la Estaca. The road ends at the parador, so if it is seclusion you are looking for, look no further. The site was chosen from a helicopter by one of Franco's ministers.

Valverde
Boomerang hotel 2 star, Doctor Gost No 1 (tel: 55 02 00). Owned by a one-time visitor to Australia, this is the only hotel in Valverde. Comfortable, not luxurious, but with a bar and restaurant.

Tamaduste
Various small apartments, owned by local people, are available for holiday lets.

Restaurants
Frontera area
The **El Castano**, five miles (8km) from Frontera and 15 miles (23km) from Valverde on a winding mountain road, specialises in grilled meat. Choose your own and have it cooked over a wood-fired grill. The Asadero or 'roastery' is set among chestnut trees and has a very rural atmosphere. Popular with locals.

Guarazoca
Local stone and wood, whitewashed walls, masses of plants and running water make it worth stopping to sit in the huge curved windows of the slightly pretentious **Mirador de la Peña Restaurant**. Marvellous views.

La Restinga
El Refugio is a family restaurant specialising in seafood and fresh fish. Mother cooks, father brings in the fish and the grown-up children serve. They also do a takeaway service of delicious avocado mojo sauce. Try also **Casa Juan** and **El Canario**.

Tamaduste
On the edge of the village with black lava fields beyond and mountains beyond those, the **Tamaduste Bar Restaurante** is cheerful and hospitable, the sort of place where the local priest comes in for lunch and watches a bit of television news as well.

Tigaday
Hostal Guanche, near Frontera on the slopes of the El Golfo basin. Here a husband and wife team serve excellent Canarian food in an outwardly unprepossessing bar.

Shopping
The **local cheese** (*quesadilla*) enjoys a high reputation. In general, though, this is an island where it is possible to be a heavy consumer.

Special Events
The **Bajada de la Virgen de los Reyes** (Descent of the Virgin of the Kings) from her shrine in the forests to Valverde. Every fourth year, first weekend in July, 1993, 1997 etc.

Sport
People come to Hierro for the **walking**. The landscape and the views are wonderful, but a real field day is assured for anyone interested in natural history or geology. For underwater exploration, the **Restinga Dive-In Centre** at La Restinga offers **diving** facilities and tuition. A shop next door sells all the gear.

LA PALMA

General Information

Full name: San Miguel de la
Palma. Size: 281 square miles
(728 sq km). 29 miles (47km)
north to south and max 18 miles
(29km) wide.
Highest point: 7,947ft (2,423m).
Population: 80,000.

Cool and green, La Palma is the
most northwesterly of the
Canary Islands. It is small, but in
any description of the island,
superlatives abound. Its centre
is a national park dominated by
a huge crater called the Caldera
de Taburiente, which is said to
be the deepest in the world. The
northern rim of the crater rises
to form the island's highest peak
at 7,947ft (2,423m). In relation to
the size of the landmass it rises

from, it is, according to
enthusiasts, the highest peak in
the world. East, north and west
of the great crater, the land
plunges towards the sea in deep
ravines. But to the south, Las
Cumbres, a ridge of lesser
volcanic peaks, makes a raised
spine running away down the
centre of the land. The Volcán
de Teneguía on the island's
southernmost tip, still
smouldering today, was the
scene of a 1971 eruption, the
most recent in the canaries.
Another striking aspect of La
Palma is the overwhelming
greenery. The gorges that fall
steeply to the sea are covered

*Greenery is everywhere on La
Palma, and even the little capital of
Santa Cruz has fields near the centre*

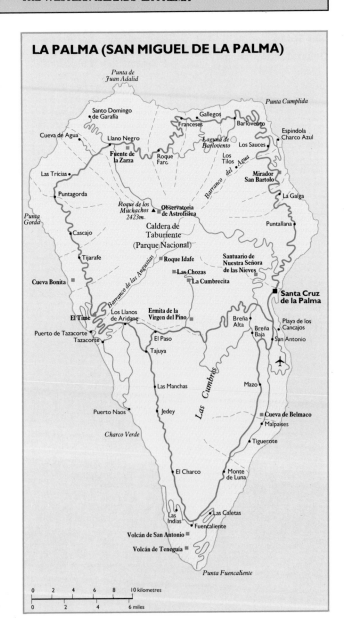

LA PALMA (SAN MIGUEL DE LA PALMA)

with dense woods of pine, myrtle and laurel. Bananas are grown on a grand scale, and avocados and tobacco are on the increase. The coast is rugged, with cliffs dropping abruptly to the sea and a few small beaches of fine black sand. For that reason, perhaps, there are no huge tourist developments on the island.

Island History

La Palma was conquered by Alonso Fernández de Lugo and became a dependency of the Spanish crown in 1493. Granted a licence to trade with America the island soon became a major commercial centre attracting entrepreneurs from the whole of Europe. In the 16th century, the capital, Santa Cruz, was regarded as one of the three most important Spanish ports, exporting cane sugar and building ships. The resultant prosperity made it a ready target for pirates like the English privateer Sir Francis Drake, who was successfully repulsed by cannon fired from the Castillo de Santa Catalina.

RESORTS

PLAYA DE LOS CANCAJOS

Three miles (5km) south of Santa Cruz, this is a recent but growing tourist development on a small, rocky bay of black sand between the airport and the city. The accommodation consists of apartment hotels and apartments, all so far on a modest scale. But the concrete mixers have not finished yet.

PUERTO NAOS

The longest-established tourist development on the west coast of the island is surrounded by lava fields and banana plantations. It is used mainly by Germans, and Spaniards visiting their holiday apartments from the neighbouring island of Tenerife. Bars and restaurants are edged by a promenade above a wide beach of black sand, planted with palms. The sea is calm with excellent swimming. **Charco Verde** beach, further south, is traditionally reserved for nude bathing.

SANTA CRUZ DE LA PALMA

Santa Cruz, or Holy Cross, was founded by Alonso Fernández de Lugo in 1493. It is small and contained within natural limits. Its most interesting old buildings can be found in the couple of streets and squares behind the long stretch of the Avenida Marítima which lines the seaward side of the city.
On the Avenida itself there are a number of charming old Canarian houses with decorated wooden balconies, among them the Parador Nacional, built in Spanish colonial style. A variety of bars and pavement cafés along the Avenida bring the city to life in the evenings.

WHAT TO SEE IN SANTA CRUZ

AYUNTAMIENTO

A former cardinal's palace of the mid-16th century, this is now the Town Hall – one of many striking historic buildings on the triangle made up of the Plaza de España and the Calle O'Daly. The exterior is arcaded Italian Renaissance but the interior is all

The arcaded Ayuntamiento of Santa Cruz was built as a cardinal's palace in the 16th century

dark Canarian wood panelling. Murals by Mariano de Cossio depict scenes of local life.

◆
BARCO DE LA VIRGEN/MUSEO NAVAL
Avenida de las Nieves
A surprising sight at the end of the Plaza de la Alameda, the Barco (Ship) is a life-size concrete replica of Columbus's *Santa Maria*, its prow facing the sea. The maritime museum in the hold of the ship is not very interesting, but it is worth going through the two floors of exhibits to emerge on the deck of the *Santa Maria* with its sudden view of the sea.
Open: 10.00–13.00, 16.00–19.00 hrs.
Closed: Saturday afternoon and Sunday.

◆◆
IGLESIA DEL SALVADOR
Plaza de España
A 16th-century church at the top of a noble stone staircase. There is a fine Moorish-style (*artesonado*) ceiling in the nave and an unusual example of Gothic vaulting in the sacristy. The impressive but non-functioning fountain beside the church was built on the site of the first Cabildo or Regional Council of the island, which in turn was formerly the meeting place of the elders of the pre-Hispanic people of the island.
Open: daily, 08.30–13.00, 16.00–20.30 hrs.

◆
IGLESIA DE SAN FRANCISCO/MUSEO DE HISTORIA NATURAL Y ETNOGRÁFICO
Calle de San Francisco
The 16th-century church is also the site of the Museum of Natural History and Ethnography. The collection was reorganised when the present king and queen of Spain paid a visit to La Palma. Exhibits include remains of Guanche artefacts, ecclesiastical vestments and treasures.
Open: daily, 10.00–13.00, 16.00–18.00 hrs.

WHAT TO SEE OUTSIDE SANTA CRUZ

BARLOVENTO
A substantial agricultural town on the northeast tip of the island. The parish church was built in the 17th century. Three-quarters of a mile (1km) west from Barlovento there are signposts to the **Laguna de Barlovento**,

officially described as the largest artificial lake on the island. It was designed as a water reservoir and will fulfil its secondary function as a beauty spot when the problem of water seepage is solved. At the moment it is a dry lake. The road to the west from this point is an unmade track but perfectly passable. It tunnels through gorges and climbs and descends through wooded hills of great loveliness. Steep tracks lead down to isolated fishing villages like **Gallegos** and **Franceses** which are little visited and untouched by tourism.

BARRANCO DE LAS ANGUSTIAS

This long gorge on the west side of the Caldera de Taburiente drains water from the crater in a series of streams and waterfalls. The name means 'gorge of anguish': it was the scene of the resistance of Tanasu, the only Guanche leader on the island who did not capitulate to the Spanish invaders. After a siege of seven months he was tricked into captivity and, refusing to eat or drink, died on his way to Spain. This is the easiest point of access for walkers in the Caldera. From here, too, it is possible to hike to the **Roque Idafe**, a monolithic basalt column, important in the religious life of the Guanches.

CALDERA DE TABURIENTE
See **Parque Nacional de la Caldera de Taburiente**

CUEVA BONITA
A seawater grotto on the west coast of the island, it is reached

by fishing boat from Tazacorte. The trip takes about three hours and operates on a fairly causal basis, depending on the weather and number of takers.

EL PASO
The silk and cigar centre of La Palma, El Paso is a prosperous town east of Los Llanos in the centre of the island. The tobacco industry is doing well but silk manufacture has declined since the 18th century when there were over 3,000 looms on the island. If there are no signs to the silk-making, ask for directions to the house of Señora Bertila Pérez Gonzales. See **Shopping**.

FUENCALIENTE
Named after the hot thermal spring (*fuente caliente*) which disappeared under the volcanic lava of the eruption of San Antonio in 1667, this town stands on the southernmost tip of the island. It is famous for vines cultivated in the volcanic ash on the hillsides around, producing the much admired Malvasía wine, or Malmsey. A short walk down from the town takes you to the crater of the San Antonio volcano, 2,156ft (657m), from which you can see the site of the most recent eruption at Teneguía, 1,440ft (439m). It is also possible to walk a route that takes you through both volcanoes.

FUENTE DE LA ZARZA
This is the site of ancient rock inscriptions of circles and loops, whose origins and significance remain a mystery. It is reached

The San Antonio volcano formed this crater in an eruption in 1667. It lies a short walk away from Fuencaliente

by a 10-minute walk along a footpath west of the village of Roque Faro in the north of the island. Ask at the village for directions. This area is the centre of goat-rearing, and beyond Roque Faro the only other human you are likely to see on this road is a goatherd with his flock, or someone gathering piles of pine-needles for animal bedding and compost.

◆
GARAFÍA/SANTO DOMINGO DE GARAFÍA

The village of Garafia (in the northwest) is often nominated by Palmeros as the most attractive on the island. It is a self-sufficient rural community with excellent fish restaurants. A rival contender for the same title is the village of **Puntagorda**, further down on the west coast. Surrounded by pines, almond trees and giant heather, it is most spectacular in the spring. The village produces almonds, flowers, potatoes and bananas.

From La Cumbrecita or Las Chozas the bottom of the crater is about four or five hours' walk away, but is not a trip to make without a guide.

◆
LOS LLANOS DE ARIDANE
The second town of the island after Santa Cruz, Los Llanos is the centre of a plain where bananas, avocados and tobacco are grown. No mean city as cities on La Palma go, Los Llanos offers wide streets lined with tulip and flame trees, a charming early 16th-century church housing the Flemish image of Nuestra Señora de los Remedios (the patron saint of the town) and some examples of grand Canarian architecture around the Plaza de España, which is shaded by beautiful old laurels. Los Llanos seems to be the natural destination for those seeking evening entertainment on the island. It has a cinema, and a couple of pubs and discos.

◆
LOS SAUCES
This comfortable town is the farming centre of the north of the island. There are bananas all over the hillsides for miles around and down to the sea. The focal point of the town is the parish church at one end of a broad open square. Substantial marble floors and columns testify to the long-established prosperity of this region.

◆◆
LOS TILOS
An area of ancient woodland, mostly of lime, laurel, myrtle trees and giant ferns, it lies along the Barranco del Agua just south of Los Sauces. This area is of

◆◆
LA CUMBRECITA
A viewpoint located as far into the heart of the Caldera as it is possible to go by road. From Santa Cruz heading west, the road leads through the Tunel de la Cumbre and winds up through pine forests. The view from the mirador at La Cumbrecita is spectacular when it is clear. But if all you can see is clouds, try the mirador a little further west at **Las Chozas**: there can be quite different weather conditions within a short distance on La Palma.

The Caldera de Taburiente is one of the world's deepest craters, and is now a national park

such environmental and botanical interest that it is under UNESCO protection.

◆
MAZO
A little south and west of the airport, Mazo is the pottery centre of the island. A workshop in an old mill, **El Molino**, displays and sells rough earthenware pots made without a wheel and decorated with the designs found on early Guanche pottery. In the same village the church, Iglesia de San Blás, is notable for its fine altar and carvings dating from the 16th century.

◆◆
MIRADOR SAN BARTOLO
The view from this lookout on a small headland north of Santa Cruz is of many deep-cut ravines covered in woods or terraced for agriculture, dotted with small white houses and falling down sharply to the rugged coast. The villages here are small and peaceful, almost deserted; the dog lying in the middle of the road will slowly shamble to the side to let you pass and only bark a warning at you when you are safely gone. Northwards through thick green banana plantations hissing with irrigation pipes is **Charco Azul**, which offers a nondescript but cheerful bar and restaurant. The village also boasts a sea-water pool, a small area protected by rocks for relatively calm bathing – the rest of the coast is very wild. The track through the same dense banana terraces continues past sheds where men trim and pack the fruit and on to the fishing village of **Espindola** with boats drawn up on a black shingley beach surrounded by

high cliffs. A large number of concrete blocks lying around the harbour make this a less picturesque place than it might be.

◆

OBSERVATORIA DE ASTROFISICA

The clear atmosphere and cloudless nights at the highest point on the rim of the Caldera de Taburiente, Roque de los Muchachos, was the reason for siting the Astrophysical Observatory here. The observatory, one of the most important in the world, is maintained by several European countries, to provide research facilities in the field of astrophysics. It is not generally open to the public without a special application to visit but you can catch a glimpse of its space-age buildings on the way to the Roque de los Muchachos.

◆◆◆
PARQUE NACIONAL DE LA CALDERA DE TABURIENTE ✓

This national park is a huge crater – La Caldera – which is over five miles (9km) across at its widest point and has a circumference of 17 miles (28km). At its highest point, at Roque de los Muchachos, it is 7,977ft (2,426m). The crater dominates the island, and its stark, bare peaks stand out from pine-covered slopes rising from laurel and myrtle woods. This is an area of great interest for botanists, geologists and zoologists, volcano-specialists and pleasure-seekers, whether walking or driving, and though

the park is small it is extraordinary. At the southeastern approach to the crater, there is a sign to the **Ermita de la Virgen del Pino**, the hermitage church of the Virgin of the Pines. The setting of this little white building in the pine-covered hillside is worth a small detour.

◆◆
SANTUARIO DE NUESTRA SEÑORA DE LAS NIEVES

In the hills two miles (3.5km) west of Santa Cruz stands the most important religious building on the island: the Shrine of Our Lady of the Snows. This small, white, 17th-century church with Canarian balconies, in a square surrounded by flamboyant trees, houses the figure of the patron saint of the island. The terracotta image, dressed in grand robes on an ornate silver altar, dates from the 14th century and is one of the oldest religious objects in the Canaries. Every five years – 1995, 2000 – there takes place La Bajada de la Virgen (The Descent of the Virgin), when the image is taken down to Santa Cruz.

◆
TAZACORTE

It was here, on 29 September 1492, that the Castillian forces under Alonso Fernández de Lugo first landed on the island. Now the town is a peaceful and industrious centre of banana production and fishing. There has been some dismal modern building but Tazacorte retains grand old 16th-century houses. The streets immediately behind the main thoroughfare are small, cobbled passages threading through the slopes of the town. There is a small beach used by locals down a side road at the north end of town by the church. Continuing north, the fishing harbour is a busy focal point, and with plans to build a swimming pool near by it looks as though it will continue to develop. Good fish restaurants are also springing up.

◆◆◆ VOLCÁN DE TENEGUÍA ✓

The most recent volcanic eruption on the island (1971) extended the southern coastline at Teneguía. The volcano is no longer active, but as you approach it, through a wild landscape of lava fields (terraced for vines) you feel the warmth in the ground through the soles of your feet.

Accommodation
Playa de los Cancajos
Apartmentos Salinas (tel: 43 43 48) is a new, smart complex of apartments attached to the proposed but as yet uncompleted 4 star hotel, **Taburiente Playa**. Facilities include a swimming pool, supermarket and disco. The **Hacienda San Jorge apartments** (tel: 43 40 75) are built to the traditional design of a local artist, and are set in gardens with seawater swimming pool, gym and sauna facilities. **Centro Cancajos** (tel: 18 13 00) are pleasant apartments around a swimming pool, **Largo Azul** (tel: 43 51 28) is very similar. **La Cascada** (tel: 43 42 80), apartments, also has a small shopping complex attached.

Santa Cruz
Hotel San Miguel, Avenida José Antonio 31, 3 star (tel: 41 12 43). Large hotel in centre of town. Often used by groups of walkers. Cheerful and friendly. **Parador de Santa Cruz de la Palma,** Avenida Marítima 34, (tel: 41 23 40). A large colonial-style house, not as luxurious as some paradors, but reliable and comfortable, with good service.

Nightlife and Entertainment
Very limited. 'Nightclub' is often the local euphemism for a place of ill repute. **Disco Aquarium** at Los Llanos de Aridane is widely regarded as the best on the island. In the same street, there is one other disco and several pubs.
Melody is a popular Karaoke bar in Puerto de Naos and, in Concajos, young ravers patronise the **Hermoteca** disco.

Restaurants
Los Cancajos
La Fontana and **Havana** are both recommended for good cooking and a pleasant atmosphere. **El Pulpo**, on the beach, may look a shack but it serves excellent seafood.

Los Llanos de Aridane
San Petronio is an Italian restaurant just outside the town, run by an Italian and Flemish couple who speak all the major European languages between them. Popular with locals.

Santa Cruz
Restaurante Canarias on the Avenida Marítima offers real Canarian food. There are many other bars and restaurants along the Avenida which come to life in the evening and where

A vortex cloud above the Caldera de Taburiente. It dominates the view from Tazacorte, a peaceful centre for banana growing

you can sit, drink and eat tapas and *raciónes*, the tasty little Spanish snack dishes.

Tazacorte

Playa Mont is an excellent fresh fish restaurant down by the harbour. Eat inside or out among the palms and papaya trees in the courtyard. Try also **Monte Cristo**. The exterior is scruffy but the food is top class.

Shopping

A frequent boast here is that the local cigars are better than Havana's. You can test that assertion at any tobacconist. La Palma and the island of San Miguel are the only two places in Spain where **silk** is still produced by traditional methods. The centre of this small cottage industry, is still in **El Paso**, but the workshop here, Casa de Sericultura (tel: 48 56 92), is more often shut than open. It seems very likely that the traditional skills of silk-making are dying out on the island.

Pots shaped by hand without a wheel and based on traditional Guanche designs are sold at **El Molino** mill in Mazo, on the east coast. This is a very small, government-encouraged enterprise. Tel: 44 02 13.

Special Events

The Festival of Nuestra Señora de las Nieves (Our Lady of the Snows), is celebrated on 5 August each year. Every five years the whole month of August is given over to celebrating La Bajada de la Virgen, the Descent of the Virgin, from her shrine in Las Nieves to the Ship of the Virgin in Santa Cruz (1995, 2000 etc). There is singing, dancing, plays performed, cannons fired, processions in the street and the whole of La Palma celebrates.

THE EASTERN ISLANDS: GRAN CANARIA, FUERTEVENTURA AND LANZAROTE

GRAN CANARIA

General Information

Size: 592 square miles (1,532 sq km). Almost circular, diameter approx 27½ miles (44km), circuit of island approx 126 miles (200km).
Highest point: Pico de las Nieves, 6,395ft (1,949m).
Population: 700,000.

Gran Canaria is the most popular tourist destination of all the Canary Islands. It is often called Las Palmas after its main city. Of the one and a half million visitors who come here each year, most head straight for the south, to the pulse and throb of the beach resorts of Playa del Inglés and Maspalomas.
Along the same stretch of coast, however, there are smaller resorts which pride themselves on the exclusivity of their clientèle. The city of Las Palmas and the mountains in the interior have always attracted discerning foreign tourists. Apart from these spots of high activity, the rest of the island is entirely Canarian. After Tenerife and Fuerteventura, it is the third largest island in the group – but it is possible to drive around the whole island, quite comfortably, in a single day. The lasting impression is one of contrasts. In shape, Gran Canaria is an almost perfect circle with the highest volcanic peaks in the middle. Forests of laurel, chestnut and pine descend to green slopes of banana plantations and farming valleys. To the west, the land falls sharply from the centre to the sea in deep *barrancos* or gorges; to the north it remains high and green and ends suddenly in steep, rugged cliffs. In the most populated part, to the south and east, the high places level down into an arid plain fringed by wide sandy beaches. The main source of income for the island since the 1960s has been tourism. The benefits are there for all to see. The disadvantages are, for some, equally obvious. Complaints that ugly, ill-conceived and badly designed resorts have destroyed parts of the landscape are heard more often on Gran Canaria than on any other island. The huge demands on the precious water resources mean that the reservoirs are nearly always empty and that wells that have been sunk deep into the earth in search of more have lowered the water table to a dangerous level. Most water is now provided by desalination plants. It is suitable for general use but not for drinking.

Island History

Jean de Béthencourt took Lanzarote, Fuerteventura and Hierro for the Spanish throne in 1405. When he attempted to subdue Gran Canaria, he failed. It was not until 1478 that the next attempt was made by Juan Rejón. He landed on the island and founded the town of Ciudad Real de Las Palmas (Royal City of the Palms) from which he set out to subdue the rest of the island.

Gran Canaria at the time was ruled by Guanche kings, or *quanartemes*, who proved redoubtable leaders of the resistance. Even when they realised the futility of their struggle, many Guanches preferred to throw themselves from high cliffs and die rather than be taken. It was not until 1483 that the Spaniards could claim they had succeeded in imposing their authority on the whole island. The next important date is 1492 when Columbus used Gran Canaria as a staging post on his first voyage to the New World. The advantages of its position in relation to the Americas, Africa and Europe, plus the growth of trade in sugar and wine exports, brought the island growing prosperity throughout the 16th and 17th centuries. However, this in its turn brought the penalty of constant attack from pirates. Las Palmas, on the coast, was a prime target. Fortresses and defensive walls to the north and south of the city proved barely adequate to the task of defence. In 1927 the Canary Islands were divided into two provinces, with Las Palmas de Gran Canaria as head of the eastern province including Lanzarote and Fuerteventura.

The sandy beach makes Puerto Rico ideal for watersports or just lounging in the sun

GRAN CANARIA

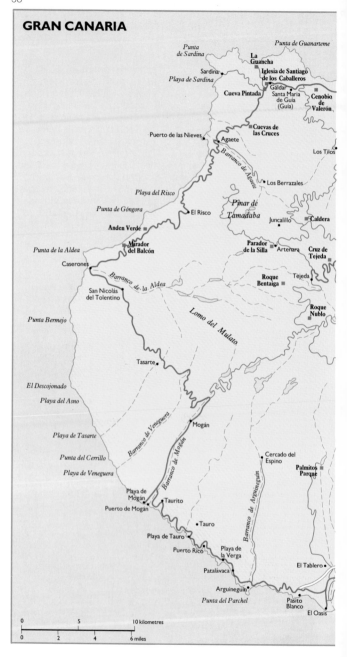

Punta de Sardina

Punta de Guanarteme

La Guancha

Sardina

Iglesia de Santiago de los Caballeros

Playa de Sardina

Gáldar

Cueva Pintada

Santa María de Guía (Guía)

Cenobio de Valerón

Cuevas de las Cruces

Puerto de las Nieves

Agaete

Los Tilos

Barranco de Agaete

Los Berrazales

Playa del Risco

Pinar de Tamadaba

Punta de Góngora

El Risco

Juncalillo

Caldera

Anden Verde

Parador de la Silla

Artenara

Cruz de Tejeda

Punta de la Aldea

Mirador del Balcón

Caserones

Barranco de la Aldea

Roque Bentaiga

Tejeda

San Nicolás del Tolentino

Roque Nublo

Punta Bermejo

Lomo del Mulato

Tasarte

El Descojonado

Playa del Asno

Barranco de Veneguera

Mogán

Playa de Tasarte

Cercado del Espino

Palmitos Parque

Punta del Cerrillo

Barranco de Mogán

Playa de Veneguera

Barranco de Arguineguín

Playa de Mogán

Taurito

Puerto de Mogán

Tauro

Playa de Tauro

Playa de la Verga

Puerto Rico

El Tablero

Patalavaca

Arguineguín

Pasito Blanco

Punta del Parchel

El Oasis

0	5	10 kilometres
0	2	4	6 miles

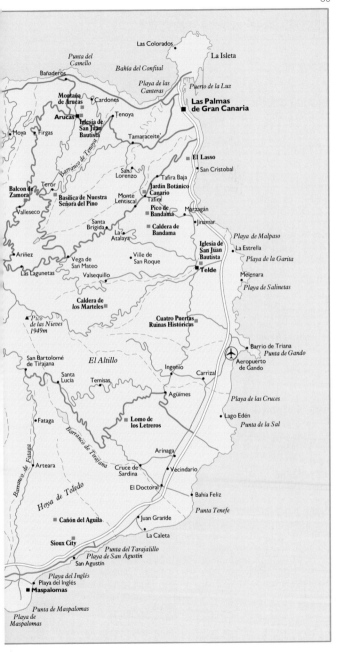

Las Colorados

La Isleta

Punta del Camello

Bahía del Confital

Bañaderos

Playa de las Canteras

Puerto de la Luz

Montaña de Arucas ▪ Cardones

Las Palmas de Gran Canaria ▪

Tenoya

Arucas ▪

Iglesia de San Juan Bautista ▪

Moya • Firgas

Tamaraceite

El Lasso ▪

• San Cristobal

San Lorenzo

Tafira Baja

Jardín Botánico Canario ▪

Balcón de Zamora

Basílica de Nuestra Señora del Pino

Terór

Monte Lentiscal

Tafira

Marzagán

Vallesco

Pico de Bandama ▪

Jinámar

Playa de Malpaso

Santa Brígida

Caldera de Bandama ▪

Iglesia de San Juan Bautista ▪

La Estrella

Ariñez •

La Atalaya

Playa de la Garita

Vega de San Mateo

Ville de San Roque

Telde ▪

Las Lagunetas •

Valsequillo

Melenara

Playa de Salinetas

Caldera de los Marteles ▪

Cuatro Puertas Ruinas Históricas ▪

▲ *Pico de las Nieves 1949m*

Barrio de Triana •

Punta de Gando

San Bartolomé de Tirajana

El Altillo

Aeropuerto de Gando

Santa Lucía

Temisas

Ingenio

Carrizal

Agüimes

Playa de las Cruces

• Fataga

Lomo de los Letreros ▪

Lago Edén •

Punta de la Sal

Arinaga

• Arteara

Barranco de Tirajana

Cruce de Sardina •

Vecindario

El Doctoral

• Bahía Feliz

Hoya de Toledo

Punta Tenefe

Cañón del Aguila ▪

Juan Grande

La Caleta

Sioux City ▪

Punta del Tarajalillo

Playa de San Agustín

San Agustín

Playa del Inglés

• Playa del Inglés

Maspalomas ▪

Punta de Maspalomas

Playa de Maspalomas

RESORTS

ARGUINEGUÍN/PATALÁVACA
*six miles (10km) west of
Maspalomas*
Arguineguín is the original
fishing village from which this
resort grew. But despite a green
centre of palms and bananas the
tourist development is so dense
that neither 'fishing' nor 'village'
are words you would now
associate with it. The cement
factory does nothing for it, either.
The white sandy beach of
Patalávaca, a little further west, is
delightful and seems to be used
as a spillover from Arguineguín.

BAHÍA FELIZ
This is the newest resort (or
'urbanisation') as you hit the
south of Gran Canaria on the east
coast expressway. The facilities
are all there – hotels, apartments,
shops and restaurants – but the
beach is decidedly black and
small. Most people swim in their
hotel pools and sunbathe on
hotel terraces. Good for
windsurfing.

LAS PALMAS
This city was a holiday
destination patronised by the
British long before any other
development on the island. Now,
as well as serving its commercial
and maritime functions, it is a
busy cosmopolitan resort, with a
dense area of hotels – some
extremely prestigious – shops,
bars and restaurants lining the
one-and-a-quarter mile (2km)
beach of Las Canteras. Offshore
reefs which form a natural
volcanic barrier make this beach

*Drinks on the promenade above the
beach: one of the many pleasures
of the Playa del Inglés*

safe for swimming as well as for
practising the various watersports that are available. Because
Las Canteras is a town beach
patronised during summer
weekends by locals, it can
become extremely crowded.
The population is also
periodically swelled by sailors.
Away from the beach area, the
historic sites and buildings of the
town are concentrated in a small
area of the old town, La Vegueta,
in the south of the city. (See also
Las Palmas, **What to See**, below.)

MASPALOMAS
Maspalomas is by far the largest
tourist development in the

Canaries and therefore in the whole of Spain. It is an amalgam of three formerly separate resorts. Running north to south, as first experienced by visitors arriving from the airport, these are **San Agustín**, **Playa del Inglés** and **Maspalomas** proper. They lie about an hour's drive from Las Palmas on the four-lane expressway down the eastern coast. Extraordinarily rapid development has occurred here since the 1960s, taking advantage of the sunny weather of the south – claimed locally as 350 days of sunshine – and over four miles (6km) of sandy beaches. At the southern extreme, these end in a peninsula of Saharan-style sand dunes, brilliant white and one of the most beautiful features of the whole of the Canaries. From the

motorway, however, first impressions are of concrete and advertisements, apartments and hotels, with regular and increasingly insistent signs to individual tourist 'urbanisations'.

San Agustín

The earliest development on this stretch of coast, San Agustín still considers itself a cut above the rest. With some important hotels, good restaurants and a quiet beach of dark volcanic sand, it deliberately cultivates a restrained and would-be classy demeanour, at least in comparison with the more robust Playa del Inglés.

Playa del Inglés

The density of hotel and apartment building is daunting until you find your way around this super-compressed tourist city. It is lively and energetic, with everything a holiday consumer might expect. Transport is efficient and easy: buses run through the resort linking beach, hotels and shopping areas. There is also an electric train called the Maspalomas Express which operates through the main streets.

Playa de Maspalomas

Separated from the Playa del Inglés by sand dunes which have been designated an official area of natural interest, this is a much smaller resort and, for some, the most elegant of them all. Certainly there are some very fine hotels here and the atmosphere is not so unashamedly boisterous as elsewhere. Tall palms and well-cultivated gardens provide a lush

The sand dunes of Maspalomas are protected from development

and restful scene. But then, before the days of tourism, this was actually an oasis.

◆◆
MOGÁN
The last resort on the southwest of the island before the road turns into the interior. Any beaches north of here are reached by long hikes or by boat. Situated some distance off the main coast road, the port of Mogán has a pleasant sense of apartness. The resort itself divides neatly into two unequal halves – the old fishing port which still operates on a rocky little beach on one side of the town, and the new, larger, purpose-built tourist development of houses, shops and restaurants around a smart and floral little marina. Almost the entire development is owned by Iberotel Club de Mar which sits on a rocky outcrop with a sandy beach on one side and the marina on the other. Most visitors are German or Scandinavian.

◆
PASITO BLANCO
on the western side of the Maspalomas lighthouse (Faro de Maspalomas)
This is an up-market private development of apartments around a marina in an attractive cove. Visitors can leave their cars and walk down to the jetty to watch the big game fishing boats unload their catch on summer afternoons.

◆◆
PUERTO RICO
some 10 miles (15km) west of Maspalomas beach
Puerto Rico has become a

byword for watersports. With a man-made beach, two lidos and a 600-berth marina in a well protected bay, this is an excellent resort for those who enjoy sailing, deep sea fishing, windsurfing, scuba diving and the like. Olympic gold medalists train at the sailing school here. There are many non-sporting visitors as well, and massive new building is taking place on both sides of the hill surrounding the original resort. On the road continuing west from Puerto Rico to Mogán, there is new tourist development round every headland, clinging to clifftops, or rising from dry river beds.

LAS PALMAS

This lively, bustling city has many roles. It is a commercial centre, one of Spain's major ports, and a considerable resort. This is where Columbus stayed on his first voyage of discovery, where the oldest historic buildings of the Canaries are to be found and where the serious cultural life of the island is lived. It has two centres, the beach and harbour at one end and the old town at the other. Each has expanded so that the two have met in the middle. The overspill is contained on land reclaimed from the sea and in a new town added on the hills behind. Walking or driving (if you can negotiate the appalling traffic) between these two major points of reference leads through most areas of interest.

The best place to start is the port. This is always a hub of activity with all sorts of vessel from many different countries.

Across the narrowest point of the Isleta peninsula, the great beach of Las Canteras stretches one-and-a-half miles (3km) to the west along a boulevard busy with bars, restaurants, shops and hotels. This is the major resort area of Las Palmas. Almost directly opposite the Santa Catalina quay in the port is the Santa Catalina park, busy enough during the day with its open air cafés and shops but coming into its own in the evening. Late at night though, this area can appear decidedly sinister. Moving further west there is the Canarian parliament building, and south of that lies the major shopping area on Avenida de Mesa y Lopez, where you will find specialist shops as well as department stores like El Corte Inglés. The beach immediately facing this area, Las Alcaravaneras, is too close to all the activities of a busy port to be recommended for swimming.

Further south through the gardens and parks of the affluent residential area of the Ciudad Jardín, you come to the Parque Doramas, a green oasis with huge palm trees and fountains. The 5-star Santa Catalina Hotel, the Néstor Museum and the Peublo Canario (Canarian Village) stand in the park. From here you can walk through busy city streets to the Parque de San Telmo with its ancient dragon trees. This forms the boundary of the pedestrianised shopping area of Triana. Every style of architecture from Spanish colonial to modernism is to be found among the buildings here. Five minutes walk down the

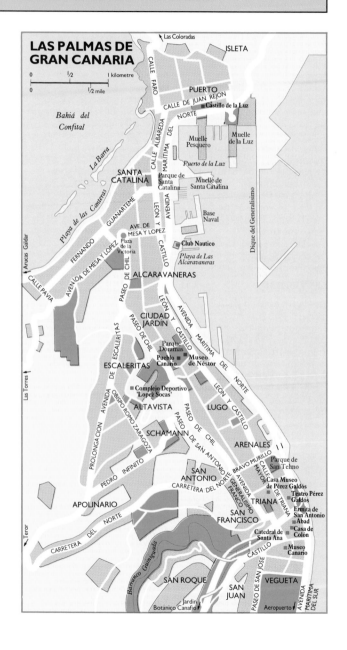

LAS PALMAS DE GRAN CANARIA

Las Coloradas

ISLETA

CALLE FARO

PUERTO

CALLE DE JUAN REJÓN

Castillo de la Luz

NORTE

Bahiá del Confital

CALLE ALBAREDA

AVENIDA MARÍTIMA DEL

Muelle Pesquero

Muelle de la Luz

La Barra

Puerto de la Luz

SANTA CATALINA

Parque de Santa Catalina

Muelle de Santa Catalina

Playa de las Canteras

GUANARTEME

LEÓN Y

AVENIDA

Base Naval

Dique del Generalísimo

FERNANDO

AVE. DE MESA Y LOPEZ

Plaza de la Victoria

CASTILLO

Club Nautico

CALLE PAVIA

AVENIDA DE MESA Y LOPEZ

PASEO DE CHIL

ALCARAVANERAS

Playa de Las Alcaravaneras

Arucas Gáldar

LEÓN Y CASTILLO

AVENIDA MARÍTIMA DEL NORTE

CIUDAD JARDÍN

PASEO DE CHIL

Las Torres

ESCALERITAS

AVENIDA DE

Parque Doramas

Pueblo Canario

Museo de Néstor

ESCALERITAS

Complejo Deportivo 'López Socas'

LUGO

ALTAVISTA

PASEO DE CHIL

LEÓN Y CASTILLO

AVENIDA OBISPO ROMO ZARAGOZA

SCHAMANN

PASEO DE SAN ANTONIO

ARENALES

PROLONGACION

PEDRO INFINITO

Parque de San Telmo

APOLINARIO

SAN ANTONIO

CARRETERA DEL NORTE

AVENIDA BRAVO MURILLO

CALLE MAYOR

Casa Museo de Pérez Galdós

Teatro Pérez Galdós

GENERALISIMO FRANCISCO

PASEO DE SAN ANTONIO

TRIANA

Ermita de San Antonio Abad

Teror

CARRETERA DEL NORTE

SAN FRANCISCO

Catedral de Santa Ana

Casa de Colón

CASTILLO

Museo Canario

Biarranco Guiniguada

SAN ROQUE

SAN JUAN

PASEO DE SAN JOSE

VEGUETA

AVENIDA MARÍTIMA DEL SUR

Jardín Botánico Canafio

Aeropuerto

0   ½   1 kilometre
0   ½ mile

Mayor de Triana across the Guiniguada ravine brings you to the **Vegueta** district of the old town. Within this small area are concentrated all the most interesting historical monuments of the city.

WHAT TO SEE IN LAS PALMAS

◆◆
CASA DE COLÓN
Calle Colón 1, Vegueta
The 'Columbus House' is a beautiful old 15th-century building, formerly the residence of the island's first governor, Pedro de Vera. Columbus stayed here in 1492 preparing for his first voyage to America, and again the following year. The house is now a museum dedicated to his travels and discoveries in the New World. It also contains paintings from the Prado in Madrid.
Open: Monday to Friday 09.30–17.30 hrs, Saturday 09.00–13.00 hrs.
Closed: Sundays and public holidays.

◆
CASA MUSEO DE PÉREZ GALDÓS
Calle Cano 6, Triana
Benito Pérez Galdós, a prolific Spanish writer and novelist, was born in this house in 1843 and lived and died here. He was a tireless advocate of social reform. The public rooms downstairs have been turned into a library and a lecture hall. Exhibits include various personal effects of the author including his death mask.
Open: Monday to Saturday 09.00–13.00 hrs.

Library open: Monday to Friday 16.00–20.00 hrs.
The writer's name is also given to the nearby Opera House, the **Teatro Pérez Galdós**, Lentini 1. This is the undisputed musical focus of the island. Every performance of any significance in Las Palmas takes place at this venue.

◆
CASTILLO DE LA LUZ
Calle Juan Réjon, Isleta
The defensive fortress beside the fishing harbour of Puerto de la Luz is the oldest historical monument on the island. It was built by Alonso Fajardo in 1494. French, Dutch and English pirates, including Sir Francis Drake, were successfully repulsed. Now, the fortress is a cultural centre, a venue for exhibitions, lectures, concerts and recitals.

◆
CATEDRAL DE SANTA ANA
Vegueta
Facing the town hall in the Plaza de Santa Ana, the cathedral was begun at the end of the 15th century but not finished until the beginning of the 20th.
The treasures of the cathedral include works by Canary artists and craftsmen like the 18th-century goldsmith José Eugenio and the sculptor José Luján Pérez. Many other examples of religious art and sculpture, and curiously enough, French porcelain, are housed in the Museum of the Cathedral (small entrance charge).
Museum open: Monday to Friday 10.00–13.30 hrs, 16.00–20.00 hrs; Saturday, Sunday 09.00–14.00 hrs.

The Parque Doramas, home of the Pueblo Canario and a museum

◆◆
ERMITA DE SAN ANTONIO ABAD
Vegueta
An 18th-century baroque church, built on the site of the first church in Las Palmas. Christopher Columbus attended mass here before he set off on his first voyage to the New World. The old streets and squares of Santo Domingo and Espiritu Santo around here are particularly attractive.

◆◆
MUSEO CANARIO
Calle Dr Verneau 2, Vegueta
The most important collection of Guanche artefacts is housed at this Museum of the Canaries. It includes domestic and agricultural tools, pottery, *pintaderas* (early terracotta seals) and carved figures. There are also 16th-century maps of Canarian towns by Leonardo Torriani and models of Guanche people and their villages. An impressive display of skulls runs throughout the length of one large room, with piles of arthritic bones. The Guanches were talented embalmers: mummies wrapped in layers of skin are displayed in glass cases, still showing hunks of hair, nails and even entrails.
Open: Monday to Friday 10.00–13.00 hrs, 15.00–19.30 hrs, Saturday 10.00–12.00 hrs.

MUSEO DE NÉSTOR
Parque Doramas
Facing the Pueblo Canario
(Canarian Village) on one side
of the square stands the house
of the modernist painter who
designed it, Néstor de la Torre.
Pleasant and light, the whole
house is a permanent exhibition
of his sketches, paintings and
theatrical set designs.
Open: Monday, Tuesday,
Thursday, Friday 10.00–13.00,
16.00–19.00 hrs, Saturday
10.00–12.00 hrs, Sunday
10.30–13.30 hrs.
Closed: Wednesday.

PUEBLO CANARIO
Doramas Parque
A re-creation of a typical
Canarian village in the grounds
of Parque Doramas by the
modernist Canarian painter,
Néstor de la Torre. It is all fake,
but a pleasant enough place to
drink sangría, buy souvenirs
and samples of local crafts, and
attend displays of folk dancing
and singing.
Performances take place on
Thursday evenings, 17.30–19.00
hrs, and Sunday mornings
11.45–13.00 hrs. Also on Sunday
mornings, keen philatelists run a
busy market and exchange of
stamps in the Pueblo.

WHAT TO SEE OUTSIDE LAS PALMAS

AGAETE
This town at the mouth of the
Barranco de Agaete is the
centre of the most fertile area of
the island, growing papaya,

coffee, mango and avocados.
About half-a-mile (1km) west,
the little port of **Puerto de las
Nieves**, once important for
shipping the agricultural
produce of the area, is now
better known for its fish
restaurants and the
extraordinary rock formation on
its coast, the Dedo de Dios
(Finger of God). The
Concepción church contains a
16th-century Flemish triptych
which is on display only during
the annual festivities of the
Bajada de la Rama – the Descent
of the Branch, 4–7 August. A
survival of the ancient Guanche
ceremony for invoking rain, the
Descent involves a daybreak
climb to the great pine forests of
Tamadaba, high above this
northern coast. Villagers bring
down branches and use them to
beat the sea for rain.

ARUCAS
*eleven miles (18km) northwest
from Las Palmas*
Arucas is the third largest town
in the island, set in lush hills of
banana and sugar cane
plantations. The rum factory
produces over 50,000 bottles a
day. The town itself is
dominated by the huge black
church of San Juan Bautista, a
neo-Gothic building begun in
1909 and finished in the 1970s.
The municipal gardens near the
church have an interesting
variety of tropical plants. The
original Guanche settlement
was called Arehucas and the hill
to the north of the town is the
scene of the final defeat of the
Guanche king Doramas, tricked
and slain in single combat.

◆◆◆
CALDERA DE BANDAMA ✓

Six miles (10km) south of Las
Palmas, the road climbs through
prosperous rolling hills and the
wine growing district of El
Monte, up to the Caldera de
Bandama – the Bandama Crater.
The views from the height of
Bandama peak 1,870ft (569m)
are beautiful, taking in the east
coast of the island, the town of
Las Palmas and, right below, the
crater: 1,100yd (1km) wide and
650ft (200m) deep. Apart from
its dimensions, there is nothing
to remind you that this is a
crater caused by a huge
volcanic explosion. All is rural
peace and quiet. The farm on
the floor of the crater is reached
by a track down the side. This
green, fertile area was much
favoured by early British visitors
who constructed the 18-hole
Bandama golf course at the turn
of the century. The first in Spain.
Neighbouring towns like **Santa
Brígida** and **Tafira** are
refreshing summering places
for those seeking cool shade in
Gran Canaria's heat.

◆◆
CENOBIO DE VALERÓN

East of Guía on the old coast
road, this network of about 500
caves is set into steep hillsides
overlooking a ravine. Signs are
inadequate and it is easy to
drive past. The purpose of the
caves is not known for sure, but
the most likely explanation is
that they were used for storing
grain.
The circle of stones on the flat
hillside above the Cenobio,
called the **Tagorer**, is where the

*The view from Cruz de Tejeda
includes snowy Teide on Tenerife*

ancient governing councils of
the Guanches met. The view of
the coast from here is superb.
Open: 10.00–13.00 hrs,
15.00–17.00 hrs.
Closed: Mondays.

◆◆
CRUZ DE TEJEDA

A popular place from which to
view the highest peaks on the
island. Reached by a route
climbing through eucalyptus,
pine and chestnut-covered hills,
this is the only place outside the
southern beaches where you

will encounter more fellow visitors than you might care for. The **Cruz de Tejeda** parador, another haunt of the early visitor in Gran Canaria, serves a leisurely lunch away from the souvenir and snack stalls. From its terrace you can see the two remarkable volcanic rocks, Roque Nublo and Roque Bentayga, which had some religious significance for the Guanches. In the distance are the snowy heights of Mount Teide on the island of Tenerife. It is possible to walk to Roque Nublo but prepare for a stiff climb.

◆
GÁLDAR

The town has a charming square, the Plaza de Santiago, a town hall and the church of Santiago de los Caballeros. The town hall is famous for the antiquity of the dragon tree in its courtyard, and the church for the font which witnessed the forced baptism of many Guanches. Otherwise it is an unremarkable place but there are several important Guanche sites outside the town. **La Guancha**, is a mile (1.5km) from Gáldar. This Guanche burial place is reached by taking a right turn along the

Sardina road from the town and following the signs. To judge by the mummies found within it, the circular area of stones was where important, perhaps royal, Guanches were buried.

◆
GUÍA
On the northwest of the island, this small town is almost an eastern suburb of Gáldar. It clings to its separate identity as a centre for locally produced cheese called *queso de flor* (goat's cheese flavoured with flowers), pottery, decorated knife handles and most importantly as the birthplace of the great Canarian sculptor Luján Pérez. His figure of Nuestra Señora de las Mercedes (Our Lady of Mercies) can be seen in the parish church of Santa Maria.

Exotic cacti are among the attractions of the Palmitos Parque

◆◆
JARDÍN BOTÁNICO CANARIO
La Calzada, near Tafira Alta
The Botanic Garden was the brainchild of a Swedish botanist. He was concerned with showing the variety of plant life in the Canaries as well as rescuing those species in danger of extinction. The plants have been grown in as natural a habitat as possible.
Open: Monday to Friday, 08.00–12.00 and 15.00–18.00 hrs; Saturday, 08.00–12.00 and 13.00–17.30 hrs; Sunday, 10.00–12.00 and 15.00–17.00 hrs.

◆
PALMITOS PARQUE
The sound of running streams and the shade of the huge palms are a sufficient incentive to visit this otherwise bare corner of the island. Five miles (9km) off the main highway at Maspalomas, the subtropical oasis and park in the Palmitos ravine is also a

fascinating wild bird and butterfly sanctuary. African crested cranes, flamingoes and honey eaters in well-designed aviaries share the park with domestic fowl and peacocks, and wild canaries chatter overhead in the palm trees. In the butterfly house, a carefully controlled environment supports a variety of butterflies. Brilliantly coloured macaws perform tricks for audiences in shows running throughout the day. This is a popular destination.
Open: daily, 09.30–19.00 hrs.

◆

TELDE
nine miles (14km) south of Las Palmas
This is Gran Canaria's second city and was formerly the stronghold of Doramas, the ancient Guanche chief. There is nothing of interest in the modern town, but the 16th-century town of narrow cobbled streets and old Canarian houses is well worth visiting, a memorial to the days when Telde was building its fortunes out of the sugar cane trade. Among the historic buildings is the 15th-century church San Juan Bautista (John the Baptist) with a beautiful carved Flemish altarpiece.

◆◆

TEROR
thirteen miles (21km) down route C-817 from Las Palmas
Set in the centre of the island, the well-preserved, graceful old Canarian town of Teror is all whitewashed houses and carved wooden balconies. It is well named 'The town of balconies'. The Basilica de Nuestra Señora del Pino (Our Lady of the Pines),

patroness of the island, stands in the centre of the town. This church was built in the 18th century to commemorate the appearance in 1481 of an effigy of the Virgin in the branches of a pine tree. For a small charge you can visit the treasury.
The Casa de los Patrónos de la Virgen del Pino stands in the square of the basilica. An 18th-century house, it is now a museum of Canarian furniture and domestic items.
Teror is well worth visiting for the landscape in which it stands. The winding mountain road, lined with eucalyptus trees, curls round small villages overlooking steep ravines.

Accommodation
Las Palmas
The city provides a great variety. Luxurious 5 star hotels include the **Meliá Cristina** on the Calle Gomera (tel: 26 80 50) and the **Reina Isabel**, Calle Alfredo L Jones (tel: 26 01 00). For a more traditional atmosphere away from the beach activities, try the **Santa Catalina**, Calle León y Castillo in Parque Doramas (tel: 24 30 40). It is surrounded by tall, cool palms in beautiful gardens. The hotel also boasts the only casino in Las Palmas.
The **Hotel Concorde**, Tomás Miller 8 (tel: 26 27 50) is just one of several hotels in town which has a game of bingo going non-stop from late afternoon till early morning.
Nearer the old town, the **Sol Iberia** (tel: 36 11 33) on Avenida Marítima del Norte is a good, functional, businesslike hotel which is also extremely comfortable.

THE EASTERN ISLANDS–GRAN CANARIA

Maspalomas area

About 80 per cent of visitors to Maspalomas book their holidays through tour operators and stay in apartment hotels. These ones cater for families and welcome children:

Barbacan Sol, Avenida Tirajana 25, Playa del Inglés (tel: 77 20 30). Comfortable, well-appointed hotel with apartments built round garden and swimming pool. Each apartment has its own terrace, cooking and dining facilities. Excellent Basque cuisine in hotel dining room.

Carolina, Las Dalias, San Agustín (tel: 76 26 42). A small, intimate hotel with quiet atmosphere, gardens and easy access to the beach.

Conventional hotels that do not provide apartment accommodation are often in the luxury class:

Meliá Taramindos, Calle Retama 3, San Agustín beach (tel: 76 26 00). Famous for its casino and permanent cabaret floor show, called La Scala. Breakfast can be taken on the terrace, buffet lunch by the pool, and dinner in the grand dining room. Definitely jacket and tie affair. The hotel's beautiful gardens lead straight on to Morro Besudo beach.

Royal Maspalomas Oasis, Maspalomas beach (tel: 14 14 48). This aptly named hotel, on the southernmost tip of the island near the lighthouse, is *the* luxury hotel of Maspalomas. It has everything, including Julio Iglesias as one of its frequent guests.

Puerto Rico

The accommodation here is mostly apartment hotels. There are children's pools in most hotels, and excursions laid on by hotels often include supervised day-trips to places of interest for older children.

Courtesy buses run every half hour for those at the top of the hill who want to come down to the beach.

Camping

There are two official sites on the island:

Guantánamo, Playa del Tauro (tel: 56 02 07). Just west of Puerto Rico, 47 miles (76km) from Las Palmas. Good shade down to the sea, with an annexe on the other side of the road.

Temisas, Lomo de la Cruz (tel: 79 81 49). Travelling south from the airport, come off at the Arinaga intersection. Eight miles (12km) from the beach but a beautiful, rural site.

Children

Most hotels have a children's pool and entertainment programme. There are bowling alleys and amusement arcades, roller skating and mini-golf away from the beach. In Playa del Inglés, **Ocean Park** provides well-supervised water slides, pools and fountains, and a huge fairground during the school holidays with all manner of rides and stalls. **Sioux City** near San Agustín has popular Wild West shows.

Culture, Entertainment and Nightlife
Las Palmas

The **Opera Festival** is held from the beginning of February to mid-March. Singers like Montserrat Caballé, Luciano

Pavarotti and Plácido Domingo perform here. The **Philharmonic Orchestra** of Gran Canaria is in residence at the Teatro Pérez Galdos, Lentini 1, from the beginning of October to the middle of June. The **Spring Festival of Music and Dance** in April–May also brings internationally known guest performers.

Nightlife and entertainment is something you do not have to look for in Las Palmas. It is everywhere, particularly in the Canteras and the Santa Catalina park area. The large hotels always have something going on and they can offer some terrific entertainment. Try **Dino's** on the top of Los Bardinos hotel, **Zorba's** on Luis Morote and **Toca Toca** on Plaza de España are recommended for young disco enthusiasts; **Utopia** pub on Calle Tomás Miller is a lively place for any age. Louder, earthier places exist, of course, and can be found with no difficulty.

In the Maspalomas area, the casino at the **Meliá Taramindos Hotel**, San Agustín, is very popular with those who want to inject a bit of risk into their lives. You can also order a proper meal, as opposed to a snack, in the early hours of the morning. The **Scala** floorshow (winters only) is a great attraction. All pink, with polished floors and lights and mirrors, seating 1,000 people to watch the dancing girls as well as top class cabaret and variety acts (smart dress required).

Most of the popular entertainment can be found in Playa del Inglés, and people from other resorts will come here for a lively nightlife.

The **Metro** precinct has folk singing and dancing on Sunday mornings. Discos are everywhere, but the most popular include **Joy**, **Chic** and **Spider**, all three in Playa del Inglés, and **Gramófono** and **Beach Club** in San Agustín.

Restaurants
Las Palmas

Casa Julio, Calle La Naval 132 (tel: 27 10 39), in the port area, is universally acknowledged as the best fish restaurant in Las Palmas. Not a pretentious place but excellent food.

El Novillo Precoz, Calle Portugal 9 (tel: 22 16 59), just behind the Playa del las Canteras. Substantial portions of meat, well cooked over wood fires in the Argentinean manner.

For a Japanese meal, try **Fuji** at Calle Fernando Guanarteme 56, parallel to the Playa de las Canteras (tel: 26 13 93) or Chinese, at **Chino House Ming** at Luis Morote 56, near the Santa Catalina Park (tel: 27 45 63). For Asturian food, try **Asturias** at Calle Miguel Rosas 5 (tel: 27 42 19). At **Pasta Real**, Calle Secretario Padilla 28, (tel: 26 22 67) there is a choice of pasta, macrobiotic and vegetarian dishes. Delicious Galician seafood is served at **O'Palleiro**, Nicolás Estévanez 31 (tel: 27 79 19). For sheer luxury, it would be difficult to beat the **Parrilla Reina Isabel,** the restaurant of the 5-star hotel of the same name, Calle Alfredo L Jones 40 (tel: 26 01 00).

Playa del Inglés
The variety of restaurants in this resort is enormous but most fall

Folk dancing at the Pueblo Canario in Las Palmas

San Agustín
The **Beach Club** at Playa de los Cocoteros (tel: 76 04 00) has an excellent restaurant serving international food by the poolside. Pleasant, elegant atmosphere. The Italian **Chez Mario** restaurant at the Urbanizacion Nueva Europa (tel: 76 18 17) is less expensive and very agreeable.

Shopping
Since the days after 1852 when the island ports were declared free with no restrictions on trade and no payment of duty, **Las Palmas** in particular has been known as a shopper's paradise. There are two main shopping centres – the pedestrianised street of **Mayor de Triana** in the south near the old town and the **Avenida de Mesa y López** near the port to the north. **Maya** is the prestigious department store in the old town and **El Corte Inglés** in the new. There are numerous bazaars, shops owned by Indian traders whose families came to the island in the last century and who now deal largely in **electronic equipment**. You will find a good selection of these shops in the streets north and west of **Santa Catalina Park** and in the **Calle Juan Rejón** by the Castillo de la Luz. Be sceptical of signs advertising a closing down sale or final reductions; and certainly prepare to bargain. You should remember the duty you may have to pay to take goods back home before you agree a final price, and make sure you know precisely what you are buying. Clever copies of expensive brand names abound. The open stalls in **Santa**

into the cheap and cheerful category.
Rias Bajas on the Avenida Norteamerica has loud advertisement hoardings outside but the atmosphere inside is much more restrained. Excellent Galician menu and a tapas bar as well. **La Toja**, another Galician restaurant, is on the Avenida Tirajana (tel: 76 11 96); in this road too is fresh Italian food at **La Liguria**. The hot bread alone is worth the visit. **La Casa Vieja**, on Carretera a Fataga, is always full of locals which is a good sign. **Bali**, on Avenida Tirajana (tel: 76 32 61) is an Indonesian restaurant much patronised by Dutch visitors.

Catalina Park sell inexpensive clothes, badly cured leather goods and tourist souvenirs. Las Palmas also has a *rastro* or **flea market** on Sundays on the Avenida Maritimo, 10.00–14.00 hrs. There is a **food market** by López Socas and Rosarito in the port area and one between Néstor de la Torre and Barcelona immediately south of Mesa y López. The oldest one is on the edge of the Old Town on the corner of **Calle Mendizabal**. In the Playa del Inglés area, there are several huge **shopping/eating/entertainment precincts** open all through the evening. For those who prefer to shop where Canarians go there is the market on Wednesday mornings and Saturdays at **San Fernando**, the local residential area immediately west of the Playa del Inglés.

For **local craft work** like basket weaving and embroidery, go to the town of Ingenio, southwest of the airport. Here you can watch the work in progress before you buy anything. The *timple*, a five-stringed Canarian musical instrument, is made at Telde and there is a pottery at Arucas. For a shop selling general Canarian craft goods, try the **Artesania Canaria Taguguy** at Calle Armas in the Vegueta district of Las Palmas.

Special Events

Local supporters say that the **Las Palmas and Maspalomas Carnival** (February/March) is second only to Rio de Janeiro – a claim also made on behalf of Santa Cruz de Tenerife. Lots of dancing and not much sleep. There are many local festivals

and celebrations like the **Bajada de Rama**, the Descent of the Branch, at Agaete on 4 August. (See Agaete, **What To See**, above). Carpets of flowers mark **Corpus Christi** in June in Las Palmas and Arucas.

Sport
Las Palmas
Surfing and windsurfing: beyond the natural barrier reef on Bahía del Confital. **Sailing**: from the two marinas of Puerto Deportivo, Calle León y Castillo and the Real Club Náutico de Gran Canaria at Puerto de la Luz.

Deep-sea fishing: excursions from Santa Catalina Pier in the port leave every day at noon. **Tennis**: at Club de Tenis de Gran Canaria at the Parque Doramas next to Santa Catalina Hotel (tel: 24 34 13), and the Club Náutico Metropole, Paseo Alonoso Quesada (tel: 24 43 46), where there are also **swimming pools** and **squash courts**.

Golf is a major sport on Gran Canaria. Closest course to Las Palmas is the Bandama Club (18-hole course), nine miles (14km) from Las Palmas on the Carretera del Centro. You can also go **horseriding** here.

Greyhound racing: at Campo España dogtrack in Calle Obispo Romo.

Cock fights take place in the López Socas Stadium from December to May. At the same stadium you can see **Canarian wrestling** (*lucha Canaraia*). Typical Canarian-style sailing boats are '**lateens**', small with large sails. See them Saturday afternoon and Sunday morning from April to September along

The Caldera de Bandama (the Bandama Crater) makes an ideal setting for golf

the Avenida Marítima.

Maspalomas area

All watersports are available in most resorts; sailing, windsurfing, scuba diving and so on. Apply to your hotel for information or contact Sun Club, Playa del Inglés (tel: 76 28 70) or Inter Club Atlantic, San Agustín (tel: 76 09 50).

Most hotels of any size provide **tennis** courts.

At the Aeroclub Maspalomas (tel: 76 24 47), you can hire light **aircraft** or go **parachuting, sky diving** and **free falling**. There is a three-hour parachuting course. Completion entitles you to free club membership. Soft landings on sand dunes at Maspalomas on Saturdays and Sundays. The **go-kart track** next to the aeroclub, for youngsters and adults, is claimed to be the largest in Spain (1,312yd/1,200m).

The Campo de Golf de Maspalomas, Avenida de Africa (tel: 76 25 81) is an excellent 18-hole, par 72 course, and the reason why many **golf** enthusiasts come to this resort. **Horse-riding** and riding lessons for the more serious are available at Picadero del Oasis, (tel: 76 23 78).

Or try a **camel safari** through the sand dunes: the address is Carretera del Faro de Maspalomas.

Puerto Rico

Renowned **watersports** facilities. Contact the sailing school – Escuela Territorial de Vela de Puerta Rico, Calle Doreste (tel: 56 07 72).

FUERTEVENTURA

General Information

Size: 688 square miles (1,731 sq km). Largest of the Canary Islands after Tenerife, but most thinly populated – 30,000. Sixty eight miles (110km) at its longest point and 19 miles (30km) at its widest.
Highest point: Orejas de Asno 2,648 ft (807m).

For modern visitors the point is the beach – miles of glorious clean white sand stretching as far as the eye can see, with small protected bays, crests of sand like mountain ridges, and golden peaks that shelve into a bright blue sea.
After that comes wind, tearing out of an equally blue sky and often threatening the pleasures of the beach. When windiest, however, Fuerteventura is a windsurfers' paradise, one of the world's leading spots for speed sailing, with possibilities for spectacular wave-sailing and, in places, plain, honest-to-goodness surfing.
So far, there are relatively few visitors to Fuerteventura, at least compared to neighbouring Lanzarote. They come in two contrasting types – seekers of peace and quiet on one hand and, on the other, the young and super-fit, clad in surfers' polychrome gear.
The island itself is extraordinary, stark and bare to the point of desperation, wind-buffeted and almost waterless. To some, aside from beach and watersports, it seems entirely charmless, well-symbolised by the fact that this is the last outpost of the Spanish Foreign Legion. The Legion's dismal barracks are one of the features of the island's dismal modern capital, Puerto del Rosario.
To others, Fuerteventura is an inspiration, with grandeur in the very bareness and splendour of evening skies that throw huge patterns of cerise and mauve across the forbidding mountains. Spain's philosopher Miguel de Unamauno, exiled here in the 1920s, described the island as 'an oasis in the desert of civilisation'.
The sand-dunes, unquestionably beautiful, are in the north near Corralejo and along the Jandía peninsula in the south. These are the island's only two substantial

A mill harvests Fuerteventura's main commodity – the wind

THE EASTERN ISLANDS–FUERTEVENTURA

resorts. Between, there lies a handful of sights worth visiting, but extremely few by comparison with any other of the Canary Islands.

This is a large island and parts of it remain rugged, inaccessible and scarcely tamed.

Island History

Arriving in 1405 to claim the island for Spain, Jean de Béthencourt is said to have remarked 'What a great adventure', '*Que fuerte ventura*'. Or perhaps it was the strong wind, *el viento fuerte* which gave the island its name.

Betancuria, in the mountains of the west, is named after the conqueror. Having overcome two separate tribes of indigenous inhabitants, Béthencourt brought in settlers from Normandy and Spain. In early days the island was more fertile and there was a considerable trade in goat hides. Apart from that, there is little to report from many centuries of hard slog. World War II, however, brought a hint of drama. Franco's Spain, though neutral in the conflict, inclined politically towards Germany. Large and extremely private German land holdings in the south of Fuerteventura brought inevitable rumours of submarine activity and it is widely believed that some war criminals made their escape to Latin America from this coast. Tourism came late to Fuerteventura but now shows signs of pulling the island, sometimes reluctantly, into the last of the 20th century.

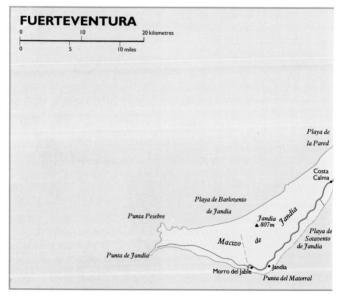

FUERTEVENTURA

Playa de la Pared

Costa Calma

Playa de Barlovento de Jandía

Punta Pesebre

Jandía
▲ 807m

Jandía

Playa de Sotavento de Jandía

Macizo de

Punta de Jandía

Morro del Jable • Jandía

Punta del Matorral

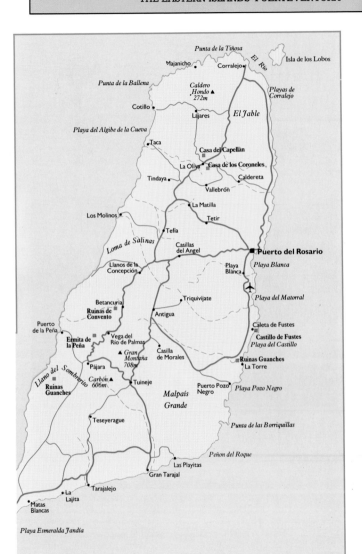

Fuerteventura is stark and bare, but it has a certain grandeur

RESORTS

The main resorts, Corralejo and Jandía, are compact, not to say dense, and are positioned to take advantage of the best beaches. Corralejo is favoured by the British and Jandía by the Germans. Other spots, some of them decidedly less promising, have recently begun a rapid development, providing a surge of time-share and apartment possibilities.

◆◆◆
CALETA DE FUSTES/EL CASTILLO

This resort south of Puerto del Rosario and the airport on the east coast is a sudden low-rise eruption on either side of a main road passing through a low-lying plain. Tucked immediately around the village's little castle and adjacent harbour, there is a pleasant complex – **La Plaza del Castillo** – with swimming pool, apartments, shops, restaurants and bars. The beach is safe and well protected, good for children.

CORRALEJO

Corralejo and Playas de
Corralejo, on the northeast tip of
the island, effectively make up a
single resort which is popular
with British and German visitors.
At Playas de Corralejo two large
hotels are sited at the northern
end of the six-mile (10km)
beach right on the sand. The
beach itself is backed by a
system of romantic and beautiful
sand dunes. The two big hotels,
the Tres Islas and Oliva Beach,
are something of an
environmental disaster; but for
those who stay in them, their
position is a source of delight.
Now, somewhat late in the day,
the dunes have finally achieved
legal protection. From the two
big hotels, new apartments
stretch north almost to Corralejo
village.

Corralejo proper was formerly
centred on its small market
square and harbour. Now a
newly built commercial centre,
the Centro Atlantico, with shops
and restaurants, has moved the
focus further down into the long
main street. From Corralejo
there are frequent ferry
crossings to Lanzarote, just
across the straits. A converted
fishing boat and a glass
bottomed boat takes day
trippers to the tiny island of Los
Lobos (see **What to See**, below).

JANDÍA

Jandía is the general name
applied to the strip of holiday
development running north from
Morro del Jable along the Jandía
peninsula almost to Tarajalejo. It
owes its position to the Playa de
Sotavento, a vast beach running
northwards from Morro del
Jable. The village of Morro del
Jable sits on either side of an old
river-bed, with a school, a
football pitch and one main
shopping street that leads down
to the sea. This represents the
older, more settled life of local
people. The new life is
represented by the busy line of
bars and restaurants along the
beach and just behind, and by
the new apartments and chalets.
Jandía itself is growing fast,
mostly with apartment hotels,
commercial centres and
restaurants. All along the road
towards the southern end of the
peninsula, deep in gullies and
high on knobs of hill, there are
also new developments, or
'urbanisations', of identical white
houses ranged in serried ranks.
The scenery northwards from
the resort is generally gaunt, but
well below the road, reached by
rough tracks downwards, there
lies the glorious fringe of beach.
This varies in width and is
protected in places by a sand-
bar, creating a lagoon-like effect.
Along the whole of its length it is
golden, brilliant and often empty.

TARAJALEJO

A small resort popular with
Spanish tourists. The
accommodation is mostly
apartments. The beach is of
black sand, unusual for
Fuerteventura. Occasionally an
effort is made to transform this
into a golden beach by dumping
truckfuls of yellow sand from
elsewhere. The effect, however,
lasts only until the next strong
wind.

PUERTO DEL ROSARIO

The present capital of the island was formerly known as the Puerto de Cabras – Harbour of the Goats – which was probably the better name. The harbour itself is quite lively, evocatively dressed Spanish foreign Legionaries sometimes direct the traffic; and that is about as far as the town goes in terms of charm and interest.

WHAT TO SEE ON FUERTEVENTURA

BETANCURIA
Founded by Jean de Béthencourt in 1405, this town was the capital of the island until 1834. Though tiny and somewhat decrepit, it has a serious and settled look, as monumental as this island gets. The site was chosen for its fertility and for its inaccessibility. It proved, in the end, not inaccessible enough.

Iglesia de Santa Maria
The church, originally a cathedral, was founded by Béthencourt and destroyed by pirates in 1539. Slowly rebuilt, it now has an 18th-century air. The interior is simple, broad and open. The gilded high altar dates from the second half of the 17th century and the ceiling has decorated beams, very typical of the Canaries.

Museo de Arte Sacro
In the basement of a building which doubles up as home of the curate, the Sacred Art Museum houses an interesting collection of photographs of all the island churches as well as vestments, carvings, and other works of art.

There is only one person to open the doors of both church and museum, a short distance away, so patience and enquiry may be called for.

Other public buildings in Betancuria include the small **Museo Archeológico** (Archaeological Museum) on the far side of the gully from the former cathedral, and a roofless and ruined **Franciscan friary** to the north of the town. South of Betancuria, villages nestle in deep valleys in the most handsome landscapes of the island.

GRAN TARAJAL
This commercial town and harbour on the southeast coast handles much of the island's tomato exports. The town, which has no tourist activity to speak of, is approached from the north through a valley dotted with date palms and tamarisk and the occasional whitewashed house, which give a very north African feel. Street names like Calle de Montevideo, and South American rhythms emanating from the bars, are a reminder of the close ties between these islands and Latin America.

ISLA DE LOS LOBOS
This tiny island, just under two miles (3km) off the coast of Fuerteventura, is reached by glass bottomed boat and a converted fishing boat from Corralejo. Guided parties take picnics and barbecues. It offers good swimming, exceptionally fine views and not a scrap of shade. Depending on sea and

wind, the northwest corner of the island provides terrifying-looking surfing for the brave and experienced.

LA OLIVA
The main administrative centre of the north of the island and, until the 19th century, its military base. The Casa de los Coroneles (House of the Colonels) dating from the 18th century, stands at the outskirts of the village. It was the grand home of the military commander of the island and now stands empty, a romantic ruin. The house is cream coloured, with an enormous black stone armorial doorway and florid woodwork balconies looking

Betancuria is one of Fuerteventura's prettiest villages

like the last crumbling defiance of the desert. The other substantial buildings in the village include the 18th-century parish church and the Casa del Capellán, the Chaplain's House, which is decorated with interesting Aztec-style carving and a new Art Centre.

♦
PÁJARA
After Betancuria, this is the prettiest village in Fuerteventura, shady, floral and well ordered. Prettiest of all is the church. Its portals are framed in Aztec-influenced statuary of rosettes with animals breathing fire out of wide open mouths. The interior of the church is charming, with a coffered ceiling and the altar screens in each of the two aisles prettily painted in simple, floral style.

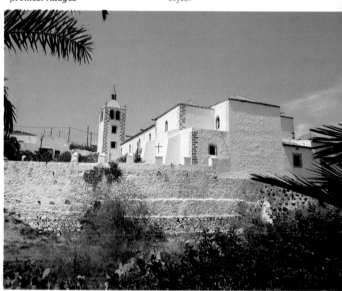

Accommodation
Corralejo
Corralejo town has mostly small purpose-built houses and apartments bookable through tour operators. Corralejo Playa has two major hotels on the beach:

Tres Islas 4 star (tel: 86 60 00). Very comfortable, with most of the facilities of a 5 star hotel – air conditioning, pool, tennis courts and a full entertainment programme. Smooth, smart service.

Oliva Beach 3 star (tel: 86 61 00). Holiday camp atmosphere in the dining room, and gives a feeling that the staff are not quite up to coping with large numbers of tour operator clients. The situation on the edge of the dunes is exceptional.

Jandía
Los Gorriones 3 star (tel: 87 08 50) is north of the resort, in a beautiful, isolated situation right on Sotavento beach with two pools, sun terraces, and gardens. Windsurf facilities and tuition are available from the F2 windsurfing school at the hotel.

Puerto del Rosario/Playa Barca
Parador Nacional **Fuerteventura**, 3 star, Playa Blanca (just south of Puerto del Rosario) (tel: 85 11 50). State-run hotel on a rather grim, grey beach, much used by local lads surfing. The parador looks like an army barracks from the outside, but bears the customary trademarks of parador style inside – comfort and quality.

Restaurants
Corralejo
La Galeria serves excellent food: delicious tapas, mushrooms in garlic, octopus in vinaigrette and a variety of fresh fish. Very good puddings too. Hawaiian cocktail bar, **Marquesina** is a good place for lunch, used by locals as well as tourists. Sit outside by the small fishing harbour and watch the windsurfers zipping about.

Tres Islas Hotel (tel: 86 60 00). À la carte menu offers an excellent choice of international and Spanish food. Elegant surroundings and good service.

Jandía
Choice is plentiful. **La Goletas** is fitted out like a ship's saloon with a lot of brass and rope and wood. Menus in German, English, Dutch, Norwegian, Swedish and Spanish, but most of the diners are German. **El Rincón** near by serves Canarian dishes. English, German, fast-food etc available.

Entertainment and Nightlife
Evening entertainments are usually available in the large hotels. There are some discos in Jandía and Corralejo but Fuerteventura is not the place for a lively night life.

Shopping
Not a leading activity on Fuerteventura. Shops in the commercial precincts of **Corralejo** and **Jandía** resorts have the greatest variety of consumer goods, from electronic equipment to designer swimwear. The larger hotels also have boutiques. At the village of **Lajares** between Cotillo and La Oliva, the **lace** and **embroidery** workshop offers its wares. Self-caterers will find all they need at Hiperfuer in Puerto del Carmen.

Beaches and climate make Fuerteventura one of the world's best watersports centres

Special Events

Each little hamlet has its own saint's day festival but on the third Saturday in September everybody celebrates the **Fiesta de la Virgen de la Peña**, the feast of the patroness of the island. There is a general pilgrimage to Vega del Río de Palma near Betancuria.

Sport

Caleta de Fustes/El Castillo provides ideal facilities for beginners to **windsurfing** and **scuba diving**.

Corralejo has rather more rigorous conditions for **windsurfing**, **scuba diving** and **mountain biking**; also **surfing** expeditions to Isla de Lobos, but only for the brave. Contact the Trade Winds Centre. Tres Islas and Oliva Beach hotels also organise **diving** lessons one day a week.

Cotillo and the beaches south of the little harbour are where the **wave sailing** enthusiasts spend their days.

Jandía, and Los Gorriones Hotel in particular, is the home of the F2 windsurfing school. Here, off Sotovento Beach, is where speed surfers try to break world records.

LANZAROTE

General Information

Size: 307 square miles (795 sq
km). 37 miles (60km) from north
to south, 12½ miles (20km) at its
widest. Highest point Peñas del
Cache, 2,214 ft (675m)
Population: 54,000

'Magical' and 'mysterious' are
words often used to describe
Lanzarote. They carry a hint that
there is something more to this
island than the beautiful sandy
beaches and year-round
sunshine that it enjoys in
abundance. Like the rest of the
Canaries, it has all the
characteristics of land blown up
from the sea bed in explosions
of fire and boiling lava. But here,
the volcanic upheavals and the
ingenious methods by which the
people have survived them
have left a landscape that is not
just extraordinary but positively
startling.

The Timanfaya national park is
now a place for tourists to gasp
at, but the eruptions in the 18th
century that produced the
Montañas del Fuego (Mountains
of Fire) were a disaster for the
islanders. Nearly a quarter of
the most fertile surface of the
island was submerged under
20–35 ft (6–10m) of lava. Many
people had no alternative but to
leave the island.

The volcanic rock from these
former scenes of devastation
comes in all colours, shapes,
textures and sizes. There are
black, red and grey craters,
fields of jagged rocks as high as
a man, grey rubble, and, in
places, a rich volcanic soil which
supports an astonishingly varied

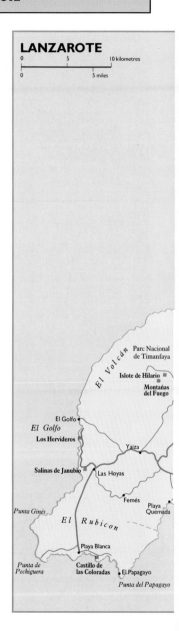

LANZAROTE

0   5   10 kilometres
0   5 miles

El Volcán

Parc Nacional
de Timanfaya

Islote de Hilario

Montañas
del Fuego

El Golfo

El Golfo

Los Hervideros

Yaiza

Salinas de Janubio

Las Hoyas

Femés

Playa
Quemada

Punta Ginés

El Rubicon

Playa Blanca

Punta de
Pechiguera

Castillo de
las Coloradas

El Papagayo

Punta del Papagayo

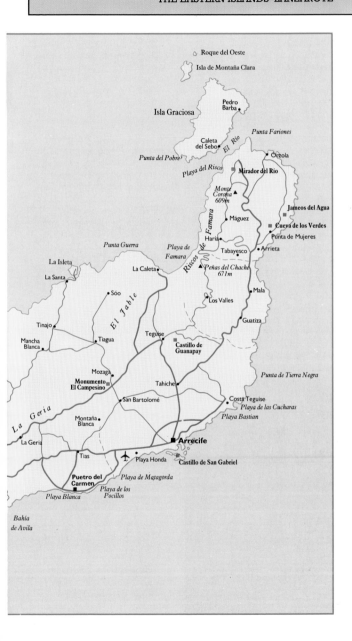

Roque del Oeste

Isla de Montaña Clara

Isla Graciosa

Pedro Barba

Caleta del Sebo

Punta Fariones

El Rio

Punta del Pobre

Playa del Risco

Orzola

Mirador del Rio

Monte Corona 609m

Jameos del Agua

Máguez

Cueva de los Verdes

Punta de Mujeres

Haría

Riscos de Famara

Arrieta

Punta Guerra

Playa de Famara

Tabayesco

La Isleta

La Caleta

Peñas del Chache 671m

La Santa

Sóo

Los Valles

Mala

El Jable

Guatiza

Tinajo

Tiagua

Teguise

Castillo de Guanapay

Mancha Blanca

Punta de Tierra Negra

Mozaga

Tahiche

Monumento El Campesino

San Bartolomé

Costa Teguise

Playa de las Cucharas

La Geria

Montaña Blanca

Playa Bastian

Arrecife

La Geria

Tías

Playa Honda

Castillo de San Gabriel

Puetro del Carmen

Playa de Matagorda

Playa Blanca

Playa de los Pocillos

Bahía de Avila

agriculture. The natural vegetation is sparse and as for trees, there are none, except palms and tamarisk.

The people live in small settlements of white houses with beautiful onion-domed chimney stacks and tidy gardens which look like car parks, covered as they are in black volcanic soil. The villages are scattered over the island wherever a living can be made out of the soil. To the north the land rises fast, then falls in sudden steep cliffs to the sea, with the islands of Graciosa, Montaña Clara and Alegranza lying straight ahead. The west coast, which includes the Timanfaya national park, is wild and rugged. The major tourist resorts lie on the eastern side of the island where the land shelves down gently into sandy beaches and coves running much of the way along to the southernmost point. From here it is just 40 minutes by ferry to Fuerteventura.

The tourist resorts are in their way as surprising as the villages. There are none of the concrete towers which characterise so many other holiday destinations, no advertisement hoardings, or electricity pylons. Having entered the tourist market later than some of the other islands, Lanzarote has learned from their mistakes. Developers strain to bend the rules governing the size and appearance of any new building, however, and sometimes succeed.

Construction now underway in the south and round the main resort of Puerto del Carmen is in places far too dense. But in general, and certainly in comparison to Gran Canaria and Tenerife, tourism is not yet spoiling the island.

The man chiefly responsible for this happy state was the late César Manrique, artist, designer, sculptor and architect of international standing. He was born on the island and strove to ensure that all new building, however modern in concept, should share the simple elegance of traditional architecture, and be in harmony with its singular volcanic landscape. The visitor arriving at the airport can see precisely what he meant. The interior of the airport was designed by Manrique.

Outside the resort areas, most

The weird volcanic landscape of Timanfaya is also known as Malpais, or 'Badlands'

people still make their living from agriculture and fishing. This, on an island with virtually no rainfall, is an achievement. The northeast trade winds bring rain to the more mountainous islands and sweep dryly over Lanzarote's low hills. The farmers, though, have discovered that the porous lava granules in which their crops are grown store the moisture of the evening dew and release it slowly during the day, as well as providing a barrier against wind and sun. So the very lava that once destroyed their living is now used to restore it. Hence the asphalt look of many fields and gardens.

This method is used to produce Lanzarote's Malvasia wine (or Malmsey) for the export market. The islanders grow onions, tomatoes, watermelon, squash, potatoes, cereals, corn and tobacco. Cochineal, a food and cosmetic colouring produced by beetles reared on prickly pear plants, is still an important export despite the modern use of aniline dyes. Fishing also plays an important part in the island economy. The waters between Lanzarote and the African coast are rich fishing grounds and Arrecife is the home of the largest fishing fleet in the Canaries.

At 54,000, the population is small but growing. Despite the arrival of tourism most inhabitants of Lanzarote remain rooted in a traditional, rural culture with a distinct and vigorous life of its own. Visitors to the island each year number about 600,000. Most of these restrict themselves to the small tourist enclaves on the coast. All the more room, then, for those who want a more enriching experience of Lanzarote, to explore the extraordinary and unspoilt countryside and meet the people.

Island History

The first recorded contact with Europe occurred in 1312 with the arrival of the Genoese sailor, Lancelloti Malocello. It is likely that he gave his name to the island. In 1402 the Norman adventurers Gadifer de la Salle and Jean de Béthencourt took the island in the name of the Spanish crown and used it as a base from which to mount expeditions against other islands in the group. When these had all been subdued, Lanzarote was left largely to its own devices and the mercies of French, English, Dutch and Arab slaving pirates. Their constant attentions explain the siting of the old capital, Teguise, right in the centre of the island, and the presence today of towers and fortifications along the coast. Up to 1837, Lanzarote remained a fiefdom of the Spanish crown. In 1730, a series of huge volcanic explosions occurred in the western part of the island. These eruptions continued for six years, destroying 77 square miles (200 sq km) of the most fertile land in the island. By 1736, a third of the island was covered with a layer of lava 33ft (10m) thick, burying 11 villages beneath it. More eruptions occurred in 1824 bringing the number of volcanoes to 29. Timanfaya is the highest crater at 1,673ft (510m) and gives its name to the national park.

THE EASTERN ISLANDS–LANZAROTE

An upheaval of another sort has been the great increase in tourist traffic to the island in the last twenty years. Visitors are mostly from Germany, the United Kingdom , Scandinavia and mainland Spain. The presence of so many people has helped to create water shortages, and there are frequent requests to be sparing in its use. Care is required, even with modern desalination plants.

RESORTS

◆◆◆
COSTA TEGUISE

An upmarket resort a few miles north of Arrecife, originally intended to attract jetsetters. The beaches on this coast though – like Las Cucharas and Playa Bastian – are on the small and rocky side. Development generally obeys the rules laid down for the island by César Manrique – low-rise, with green, blue or brown paintwork. But the further away from the smartest part, the more the resort sprawls into unfinished 'urbanisations' with apartments only half full and empty shopping precincts to let. There are bars, restaurants, supermarkets, watersports facilities, an aqua-park and an 18-hole golf course. Costa Teguise will never be as crowded as Puerto del Carmen, nor as animated.

◆◆◆
PLAYA BLANCA

Originally a small fishing village in the southwestern end of the island, its periphery is rapidly

Puerto del Carmen is Lanzarote's most popular resort

being transformed by more and more tourist building – hotels, apartments and apartment hotels, many of them at some distance from any beach. The area immediately behind the small, sandy beach in the middle of town retains a pleasant atmosphere, with bars and restaurants on the promenade. There is a marina for pleasure craft as well as a busy quay for the ferry (5 times daily) to Fuerteventura. An eastwards turn outside Playa

Blanca directs you to El Papagayo. Follow this on to a dusty untarred track which leads to the most stunning and uncrowded beaches on the island. **La Caleta** is the unofficial but widely accepted nudist beach and **Playa de Papagayo** is the most popular.

◆◆◆
PUERTO DEL CARMEN
This little harbour settlement just south of Arrecife has expanded northwards along a series of beaches to become one of the major resorts of the Canary Islands. Sixty per cent of all holidaymakers on the island are based here. There are some larger hotels on the beach near the town but much tourist accommodation is found behind the numerous small-scale shopping centres, locally known as *arcades*, which run almost the length of the Avenida de las Playas. The arcades have shops, restaurants and snack-bars by the hundred and plenty of pubs and discos. But though it is sprawling, populous and cheerful, there are no high-rise buildings at all and a considerably calmer atmosphere than at comparable

resorts on the other islands. Although the beaches all merge into one five-mile (8km) stretch of sand, it is convenient to distinguish between different stretches. The first, going west from the harbour in the direction of the airport, is now known as **Playa Blanca**. It was given this name in a promotional spirit and is all too easy to confuse with the resort of Playa Blanca on the south coast (see above). Playa Blanca (Puerto del Carmen branch) is the nearest beach to the centre of town, the most popular and the most crowded. The next beach, **Los Pocillos**, is much quieter, largely used by locals at the weekends. Here the large hotels begin again and there is less impression of a busy, holidaymakers' seafront. The resort flows north towards the airport, to a new urbanisation backing the lovely wide beach of **Matagorda**. Although not strictly in Puerto del Carmen, further along the coast beyond the airport, **Playa Honda** is now largely a residential area for locals.

ARRECIFE

Arrecife has been the capital city of the island since 1852 and is the home of more than half the population. It is also the only place in Lanzarote where you will experience a traffic jam. This busy commercial centre is built round a couple of harbours protected by extensive offshore reefs – 'arrecife' means 'reef'. The harbour to the north, Puerto de la Naos, is where the really serious business of fishing and fish processing happens. There is a wide promenade along the

sea front planted with attractive gardens, the **Parque Municipal**, and the small town beach of **El Reducto**, pleasant enough to look at but not recommended for swimming.

Arrecife is not old and its historic buildings are few. But it does have one interesting natural feature – a lagoon, Charco de San Ginés. This hardly makes Arrecife the 'Venice of the Atlantic', as some writers of tourist literature like to have it, but the lagoon, known to locals as 'The Puddle', is bordered by restaurants and shops in a very attractive setting.

WHAT TO SEE IN ARRECIFE

CASTILLO DE SAN GABRIEL

The castle is on a tiny offshore island reached by either a road bridge or an older foot bridge. At the centre of the latter is a tiny drawbridge called the Puente de las Bolas or Bridge of the Balls (there are two cannon balls on top of columns). The fortress was built in 1590 by the Italian architect Leonardo Torriani to defend the town from pirate raids. Now it serves as a small archaeological museum.

◆◆
CASTILLO DE SAN JOSÉ/MUSEO INTERNACIONAL DE ARTE CONTEMPORÁNEO

Beyond the deep-water fishing port at the north end of town, this little castle was built in the 18th century on the orders of King Philip II, to provide work for the islanders. Once built, it was used as a munitions store. Its

Visitors walk from Arrecife over a tiny drawbridge to the Castillo de San Gabriel

present and more noble function is as the International Museum of Contemporary Art, the brain child of the Lanzarote artist and architect, César Manrique. He rescued it from dereliction in the 1960s and with a grant from the government began to buy important contemporary works. You will find paintings and sculptures by Picasso and Miró, and by César Manrique himself here, beautifully lit and displayed against a background of dark volcanic walls. Below the museum, a restaurant, also designed by Manrique, offers sweeping views of the harbour entrance and the sea.
Open: daily 09.00–midnight. No admission charge.

◆
IGLESIA DE SAN GINÉS

The church of the patron saint of the island is not particularly grand but, like all Canarian churches, it is well proportioned. It has a lovely Moorish-style (*artesanado*) ceiling. Like many Canarian churches, it is in the middle of restoration after long years of neglect. It stands with its back to the lagoon of San Ginés, at one end of a square where old men sit on shady benches.

WHAT TO SEE OUTSIDE ARRECIFE

◆◆◆
CUEVA DE LOS VERDES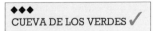

A network of underground tunnels and caves at the foot of the Corona volcano which connects with those at the

Jameos del Agua, to the
northeast of the caves. It takes
about two minutes to drive from
one to the other. The guide takes
you on a half-mile (1km) *son et
lumière* trip through tunnels and
caves created by the eruption of
the Corona volcano. The outside
crust of the rivers of molten lava
cooled and solidified while the
boiling mass inside continued its
way on downwards to the sea,
leaving hollow passages where it
flowed out. Through the
centuries, they have been a
place of refuge for islanders
against pirate attack. Now the
caves are mainly a tourist
attraction. One of the
subterranean chambers is used
for concerts, with seating for
1,000 people. Apparently the

acoustics are superb. There is
also an optical illusion – to
describe it is to destroy its effect
– which in itself is worth a visit.
Tours on the hour, daily, 11.00 –
19.00 hrs.

EL GOLFO
This is a lagoon of brilliant
emerald green in the rim of half a
volcanic crater, the other half of
which is submerged in the sea. It
is on the western edge of
Timanfaya national park, and
steep cliffs of black, red and grey
offer a startling contrast with the
bright green of the lagoon. The
intensity of colour is caused by
the effects of algae in the water.
Due to evaporation, the salt
content of the water is highly
concentrated. From the lagoon, a
black, gravely beach shelves
steeply down to the ocean.

*Haría is a traditional summer
retreat for islanders*

FUNDACIÓN CÉSAR MANRIQUE

The home of Lanzarote artist César Manrique, in Tahiche 6km north of Arrecife, was opened in 1992 after his death. It houses a collection of his own paintings and sculptures. The lower part of the house has been built into an ancient lava bed. The cave-like rooms are actually volcanic bubbles created by the eruptions of 1730–36.
Open: Monday to Friday 10.00–14.00 and 16.00–19.00, Saturday 10.00–14.00 hrs.

◆ HARÍA

A village in a valley of a thousand palms, and a source of great pride for people who are all too aware of the lack of trees on the island. Haría, nine miles (15km) northeast of Teguise, with its low white houses scattered in the cool green valley, has the look of a North African town. Traditionally it has been a popular place for islanders to retreat to in the summer. Two-and-a-half miles (4km) south of the village a mirador offers views of the valley of Tabayesco below and the villages of Arrieta and Punta de Mujeres.

◆ ISLA GRACIOSA

An island separated from the northern tip of Lanzarote by the narrow strait of El Río. There is a crossing from Orzola on the north of Lanzarote to Caleta del Sabo each morning and afternoon in the season, according to demand. The island has no tarred roads, no cars and no shade. But it does have wonderful empty beaches and sand dunes and, at the small fishing village of Caleta del Sabo, food, drink and a pension.

◆◆ JAMEOS DEL AGUA

The same lava stream which created the Cueva de los Verdes finally met the waters of the Atlantic at this point, one mile (2km) away. At the improbable juncture, César Manrique has created an underground complex of lagoon/restaurant/nightclub/tropical garden and swimming pool. A wooden staircase leads down to a large underground cave with an opening to the sky which barely provides enough light to reveal the small sea water lagoon at your feet. The floor of the lagoon is dotted with white specks – blind white crabs usually found in the ocean at depths of below 10,000ft (3,000m). You climb some steps to the nightclub/restaurant and then emerge into the brilliant sunshine and palm trees of a rocky tropical garden.
Open: daily 11.00–19.00 hrs, Tuesday, Friday and Saturday 19.00–03.00 hrs at a higher entrance fee. Tel: 83 50 10.

◆◆ JARDIN DE CACTUS

Gautiza, 17km north east of Arrecife, boasts a cactus garden so brilliantly devised that it is almost an architectural cactus amphitheatre.
Open: daily 09.30–18.00 hrs

◆ LOS HERVIDEROS

A mile (2km) from El Golfo, the wild ocean pounds into sea-caves, at a point where boiling lava and Atlantic Ocean have met to create a tormented rockscape. The name means 'Boiling Springs'. There are stopping places for cars, with walkways down specially constructed steps at various vantage points offering views of the sea raging in the rocks.

◆◆
MIRADOR DEL RÍO

This lookout point, set into the top of the high Riscar de Famara (Famara Cliff) on the extreme northerly point of the island, was built on the site of an earlier watch tower. The dreaded view then was of pirate ships on the horizon. Now, from a height of 1,475ft (450m) you see cliffs falling away sharply beneath to the Playa del Risco and the tiny multi-coloured squares of salt pans far below, the narrow strait of El Río and the island of Graciosa, edged by brilliant sandy beaches. Beyond that lie the little islands of Montaña Clara and Alegranza. The view to the west side of the island is of the Famara cliffs falling down to the coast below, the long stretch of Famara beach and the fishing village of Caleta. The mirador, with white curved walls, wooden floors, rocks, plants and nothing to distract you from the view, is perfect. *Open:* daily 11.00–19.00hrs.

◆
MONUMENTO EL CAMPESINO

near San Bartolomé
This Monument to the Rural Worker, almost in the dead centre of the island, is a tribute by César Manrique to the skill

and ingenuity of peasants who won back a living from the devastated earth. The sculpture itself is rather like a totem pole of white blocks, and at 50ft (15m) high is visible from some distance. The Casa del Campesino beside it is an old farmhouse, now renovated and housing a museum of rural life through the ages. The restaurant round a courtyard serves local food and wine. *Open:* Monday to Friday 10.00–17.00 hrs. Weekend 10.00–19.00 hrs.

◆◆◆
PARQUE NACIONAL DE TIMANFAYA

The volcanic eruptions that devastated the island in the 18th century created an extraordinary landscape, which has been a national park since 1974. It covers 20 square miles (50 sq km). The highest crater is Timanfaya, 1,673ft (510m).
The park is now a national asset, but its creation was a national disaster. The parish priest at the village of Yaiza, Andrés Lorenzo Curbelo, described the first explosions in the evening of 1 September 1730 as a mountain rising out of the earth spewing flames which continued to blaze for 19 days. Those were the first days of volcanic activity which lasted for six years and buried 11 villages.

Montañas del Fuego

The 'Mountains of Fire' are the principal attraction of the national park. Entering from the village of Yaiza, the road passes through a level landscape of tormented black rock which then turns into a desert of loose black cinders. A horned devil holding a fork, the emblem of the park, stands on guard. In the distance the red and grey flanks of the craters rise out of the ground. The conducted bus tour of the Mountains of Fire begins at the Islote de Hilario, once the 'desert island' of the hermit Hilario and now the central reception point of the park. The hermit in question apparently set up residence here after the eruptions were over, planting a miraculous fig tree on the spot. A withered tree, now incorporated into the useful Restaurante del Diablo (Restaurant of the Devil), does indeed stand on this spot but its provenance is uncertain. To demonstrate the heat within the mountain – 750°F (400°C), an attendant pours water into a pipe inserted in the earth and beats a hasty retreat: five seconds later a great blast of steam whooshes out of the pipe. Dry scrub laid in a crevice on the ground goes up in flames. For a culinary demonstration at the restaurant, steaks are grilled over an open well. Beneath lies the natural furnace of the volcano, an awe-inspiring and unlimited source of free heat. The **Ruta de los Volcánes** is a theatrical experience of the volcanoes. Taped commentaries with appropriately lunar music explain the origins of the landscape as you pass among cones and craters. There are also camel rides through selected areas of the park. These are extremely popular, and only early arrivals will avoid a wait. *Open:* daily 09.00–17.00 hrs.

You can camel-ride in comfort through the moonscape of Timanfaya

SALINAS DE JANUBIO
On the west coast, at the southern end of Timanfaya national park, the Janubio Saltpans lie in the flat base of an old crater beside an enclosed lagoon. The sea water is pumped into the many rows of square pans and evaporated to leave little mounds of white salt. Lanzarote produces 10,000 tonnes a year, much of it for use in fish processing but some for table salt. Old broken down windmills are a reminder of former, less automated days of water-pumping.

TEGUISE
This ancient capital of the island lies five miles (8km) northeast of

Mozaga. It was founded by Maciot de Béthencourt, nephew of Jean de Béthencourt, the original Norman conqueror of the Canaries. Despite repeated pirate attacks, the town has many fine old buildings.

The restored 15th-century church of San Miguel stands in the main square of the town. Facing it is the Renaissance façade of the Palacio de Spinola built in the 18th century by an Italian merchant, Vincente Spinola. It is restored and open to visitors. Other notable buildings include the 18th-century Convento de Santo Domingo and the 16th-century Convento de San Francisco, the latter in process of restoration. Teguise is the home of the *timple*, a Canarian stringed musical instrument, like a miniature guitar. You may have to look hard to find one because the tourist shops in the town stock only souvenirs of the most banal nature. On Sundays, there is a market in the square and displays of folk dancing and singing.

Outside the town but clearly visible from it is a castle, **Castillo de Guanapay**, sometimes called Castillo de Santa Bárbara. It stands on the rim of a crater, Montaña Guanapay, and was first built in the 14th century by Lancelloti Malocello, the Genoese who probably gave the island his name. Plans to build a small military museum in the castle have not yet materialised but the view is worth the walk up from the town.

TIMANFAYA
See **Parque Nacional de Timanfaya**

YAIZA
This village just south of the Timanfaya national park is generally regarded as the prettiest on the island. It has some fine old houses and the 18th-century church of Los Remedios, a couple of good restaurants and an art gallery showing the work of local artists. The gardens brim over with hibiscus and geraniums.
Galerie Yaiza open: daily 17.00–19.00 hrs.

Accommodation
Costa Teguise
Meliá Las Salinas 5 star (tel: 59 00 40). Luxury hotel on Las Cucharas beach, main entrance leading into a tropical hanging garden with pools and waterfalls. The beach is semi-private and well sheltered. The hotel provides various sporting activities such as bowling, archery, tennis and windsurfing free of charge to residents.

La Santa (near Tinajo)
Club La Santa (tel: 84 01 00) in itself is almost a resort. The logo makes a bold claim – 'No 1 sports resort in the world' and certainly no one lies on the beach here unless they are doing press-ups. The perfect place for sports and fitness enthusiasts, this hotel on the west coast of the island offers excellent facilities, tuition and coaching, all included in the price of the booking. You can windsurf, play squash, tennis, badminton, or volleyball; there is a gymnasium, athletic stadium and an Olympic-size swimming pool. Daley Thompson and other world-class athletes have trained

here. Families are welcome and there are excellent facilities for children, plus the usual bars, restaurants, shops, supermarkets, and discos.

Playa Blanca
Hotel Lanzarote Princess, Costa Papagayo (tel: 51 70 11). This spacious hotel has bedrooms built around its swimming pool area with views out to sea. Ten minutes walk from the main Playa Blanca beach, it is cheerful and comfortable, ideal for families. Sports facilities include tennis, volleyball and squash.

Puerto del Carmen
Lanzarote Palace 4 star, Playa de los Pocillos (tel: 51 24 00). Comfortable, with a large swimming pool and sun terrace area, bars, choice of restaurants, gymnasium with resident instructor, live entertainment for children as well as adults and a friendly atmosphere.
Los Fariones 4 star (tel: 51 01 75). Set just south of the Playa Blanca beach and handy for the harbour/downtown district. This is one of the old hotels and has a beautiful mature garden of palms of many kinds. Recommended and not to be confused with the same company's new and over-large apartment hotel, **Los Fariones Playa** just next door.

Entertainment and Nightlife
In both Costa Teguise and Playa Blanca, evening entertainment programmes are usually initiated by individual hotels. They include cabaret acts, flamenco dancers, competitions, discos, all at varying levels of professionalism.
The same goes for major hotels

in Puerto del Carmen but there the choice is considerably increased by clubs, pubs, bars and discos in the harbour and old town, as well as in the arcades on the Avenida de las Playas.
For bars with live music in Puerto del Carmen, try **Amadeus**, **Charlie's Bar** and **Diamond** in the arcades along the Avenida de las Playas. For livelier action and noisier music, try the **Waikiki Beach Club** or **Rock Café**, **Paradise Disco**, the **Joker**, **Dreams** and **Moonlight Bay** nightclub are all popular with the young.
If you want to drink English bitter or eat British-style beans on toast and scrambled eggs, try **Oliver's Bar** in the old town. English rules apply – pay as you order. Norah's bar, **The Dubliner**, also in the old town, is always crowded.

Restaurants

Arrecife
Castillo de San José (tel: 81 23 21) The walls of this restaurant beneath the Museum of Contemporary Art are hung with pictures. The decor is simple and elegant, the views are stunning and the food is excellent.

Costa Teguise
La Chimenea, Playa de las Cucharas (tel: 81 47 00). International cuisine in an attractive setting on the Playa de las Cucharas. Excellent service. Not cheap. Closed Sundays and month of July.

Puerto del Carmen
El Sardinero A popular fish restaurant on the harbour in the

old town. You can choose your own fish – but the later you leave it, the more likely you are to be left with just sardines. The decor is functional rather than elegant but the waiters are cheerful and so are the diners.

La Bohême, on the Avenida de las Playas, serves international cuisine in an elegant atmosphere. Paintings on the wall and antiques where there is space for them. Not cheap.

O'Bota Fumeiro, a Galician restaurant near the San Antonio Hotel towards Play de los Pocillos, serves delicious fresh seafood.

Teguise

Acatife Beautifully situated in the main square of Teguise, this restaurant serves both international and Canarian food. Try the excellent local dishes and drink the local wine. The meat is charcoal grilled. Closed Sundays and Mondays.

Yaiza

La Era (tel: 83 00 16). A restaurant in the country with a reputation for serving real Canarian food with verve and charm. Small dining rooms are set round a floral courtyard. The old photographs on whitewashed walls, checked tablecloths and rush seat chairs give it a comfortable farmhouse look. The menu cover was designed by César Manrique. In a village full of flowers, the garden around this restaurant is positively choking with them.

Shopping

Most of the shops on the island are to be found in the **arcades** beside the Avenida de las Playas, Puerto del Carmen, and in the town itself. No great surprises. Some of the embroidered cloth 'from the Canaries' has actually just come off the plane from Taiwan. But it is fun to look.

Special Events

The February/March **Carnival** is a big event on the island, as is **Corpus Christi** in June. Instead of the carpets of flowers seen on the other islands, patterns of coloured sand are used to decorate the ground. In August everybody celebrates the feast of San Ginés, the patron saint of the island. Each town or village also celebrates its own saint's day. The **Fiesta de la Virgen de los Volcánes** on 15 September in the village of Mancha Blanca, district of Tinajo, marks a miraculous deliverance from the eruption of Las Quemadas volcano in 1824. The lava headed straight for Mancha Blanca. Terrified, villagers took their image of the Virgin to confront the molten flow, which was immediately diverted.

Sport

Most hotels provide a **pool** and **tennis courts** and have access to **watersports** facilities: windsurfing, sailing and diving. On Costa Teguise, there is an 18-hole **golf** course, about a mile (1.5km) from the hotel Meliá Las Salinas. Golf clubs can be hired. At Puerto del Carmen, the Insular Sports Club (near Los Fariones Hotel) has **swimming pool**, **tennis** and **squash courts**. The Castellana Sports Club specialises in **aerobics** and **weight training**. There are four **diving** schools at this resort.

PEACE AND QUIET

Wildlife and Countryside on the Canary Islands
by Paul Sterry

For many people, the Canary Islands conjure up images of blue skies, warm seas and sandy beaches, together with the usual tourist infrastructure of hotels and bars. However, there is another, far wilder side to the islands, and within a few miles of many of the tourist spots you can reach ancient lava flows, sulphurous volcanic cones and even snow-capped mountain tops with plants that would look equally at home in the Alps. The seven main islands vary from the semi-desert moonscape of the eastern isles like Lanzarote to the lush, humid western islands like La Palma. The islands have been influenced by man for centuries, but despite a great deal of tourism and development today, many areas have been set aside and protected. There are national parks on Lanzarote, Tenerife, Gomera and La Palma, and 60 other nature reserves. The Canaries have an immense plant list, totalling nearly 2,000 species of flowering plant alone. Due to the early separation and isolation of the islands, many of the plants are found nowhere else in the world, an honour also shared by seven of the islands' bird species.

Lanzarote

Together with Fuerteventura, Lanzarote is the easternmost island in the Canaries and the closest to the African mainland. Although not as mountainous as some of the other islands, the highest point being 2,214ft (675m), the landscape is bleak and forbidding. It is dominated by the rugged hills and cliffs of Famara in the north which merge into the plains and dunes of the south.

The landscape is volcanic, with craters and cinder deserts, but somehow the inhabitants still manage to grow crops. However, despite patchy development, the terrain is largely unspoilt and has rare and interesting birds. Houbara bustards (a globally endangered species) and black-bellied sandgrouse are typical desert species which find the hostile environment much to their liking. For the botanist, the northern half of the island is undoubtedly the more rewarding, and especially

The mighty Echium wildpretii is an immense viper's bugloss which may be seen on Teide

PEACE AND QUIET

Succulent Senecio kleinia is well adapted to dry, salty conditions on Fuerteventura

the rugged Famara region. From the town of Haría you can explore the area and find a wide variety of endemic plants. The coastal cliffs support the fleabane *Pulicaria canariensis* and the daisy-like shrub *Astericus schultzii* with its pale yellow flowers, both of which are found here and on Fuerteventura but nowhere else in the world. However, the dominant plants of the coast of Lanzarote are the succulent spurges (*Euphorbia* species) and stonecrop-like family of *Aeonium*.

The cliffs provide dramatic views and seascapes, and from the northernmost viewpoint, Mirador del Río, you can look north towards the islets of Graciosa, Montaña Clara and Alegranza, breeding sites for little shearwaters and Bulwer's petrels. The dashing Eleonora's falcon also breeds around the coast and its aerobatic skills make it easy to identify.

In the south of the island lies the Parc Nacional de Timanfaya, near the town of Yaiza. The park protects the most spectacular area of volcanic activity on the island with the highlight being the Montañas del Fuego. The whole area has a distinctly sulphurous smell to it and much of the scenery was created in a violent eruption in 1730. Because of the dangerous terrain, special tours and coaches are arranged to guide visitors to the best craters and lava flows, and individual sightseeing is discouraged.

Fuerteventura

Fuerteventura is rather arid and barren. Most of the island is covered by rocky plains, although it also has fine sandy beaches, particularly in the north.

The botanical interest of

PEACE AND QUIET

Fuerteventura is centred around the northern town of La Oliva and the southern peninsula of Jandía. Dominated by a volcanic cone, dunes make up most of the north of the island, the plants that grow here face the same problems as coastal plants everywhere, namely the salt-laden air, the drying sea breezes and well-draining soil. Many of the plants are prostrate in form and include the colourful vetch *Lotus lancerottensis,* but succulents like *Senecio kleinia* are also common. Although the latter species is related to ragwort, its shrubby appearance makes it difficult to imagine anything less like the common European weed.

In the south of the island lies the rocky peninsula of Jandía, dominated by a volcanic ridge running down its spine. On either side of the ridge, the rock shelves into the sea and forms sandy beaches. In addition to the widespread succulents, several rare endemic plants are found along the coast including the spurge *Euphorbia handiensis*, while on the slopes above, the straggling viper's bugloss *Echium handiensis* can be found. This is the only place in the world where it grows.

Fuerteventura is a good island for the birdwatcher. Most of the species found here are adapted to a desert life and many, like the houbara bustard, cream-coloured courser and black-bellied sandgrouse are also widespread in north Africa. Fuerteventura is also host to two birds endemic to the Canary Islands. The Canary Island chat is like a pale version of the European stonechat; Berthelot's pipit is like a pale, grey meadow pipit. Both are probably descended from their more widespread relatives from Europe and isolation from the mainland has encouraged this process. Cultivated fields around the coast may sometimes attract these species but here you are more likely to find trumpeter finches, with their ridiculous trumpeting calls and stubby red beaks, and lesser short-toed larks. The pale, washed-out plumage of the larks gives them good camouflage as they feed along the furrows in the fields.

Gran Canaria

From Gran Canaria's central dome-like plateau, gorges and valleys radiate down to the sea and there are numerous volcanic cones which dot the landscape. Extraordinary succulent plants, like the endemic spurge *Euphorbia canariensis*, grow out of barren soil and rock and add to the scenic attraction of the landscape. With their swollen stems they could easily pass for cacti and look like rows of organ pipes.

Because of the prevailing northeasterly trade winds, the north side of the island is more humid and was formerly cloaked by evergreen laurel forests. However, centuries of exploitation by man have reduced the forest to remnant woodlands such as those at Los Tilos near Moya. Although the woods are no longer extensive enough to support long-toed or laurel pigeons, the ground vegetation is interesting, with Canary willow growing on the valley floor, while the slopes are covered with endemic laurels and holly.

In the centre of the island lies the plateau of Cruz de Tejeda which, although reaching an altitude in excess of 4,910ft (1,500m), is still accessible by road. Berthelot's pipits are common near the summit and feed in the open ground. Their song is sometimes delivered in flight when they share the skies with plain swifts (plain is the name of the type) hawking for insects. The mountain flowers are also good on the plateau

Euphorbia canariensis is at home in near-desert conditions

with succulents like *Aeonium simsii* and the shrubby *Cheiranthus scoparius* the latter a crucifer with delightful mauve flowers. The forests of Canary pines on Pinar de Tamadaba, in the northwest of Gran Canaria, are also well worth exploring. The rare and endemic blue chaffinch frequents the trees together with great spotted woodpeckers, and rock sparrows haunt open, rocky outcrops. Rock roses and asphodels are common in open areas under the pines, and the abundant, shrubby, *Micromeria pineolens* adds a splash of colour with its pink flowers.

If you have time to spare, do not miss the Jardin Botánico in Tafira, near the capital. It holds examples of many of the endemic flowers, some of which are very difficult to find in the wild.

Tenerife

The main geological feature of Tenerife is the ridge of hills which runs down the spine of the island, dominated by the volcanic peak of Teide, highest mountain in the islands. From the ridge and peaks, ravines run down to the sea and to the north, steep cliffs are pounded by the sea, while in the south the flat, coastal plain forms beaches. Seabirds can be seen from almost any promontory along the north coast. Early mornings and late evenings are best, especially when an onshore wind is blowing. Cory's and little shearwaters and the all-dark Bulwer's petrel are frequently seen, particularly during the summer months.

PEACE AND QUIET

The north coast of Tenerife is also extremely good for flowers, with the two main centres of interest being around Teno in the northwest and around Anaga in the northeast. The cliffs at Teno are dominated by succulent spurges, and many of these species of *Euphorbia* look more like cacti than European plants. This is not just a coincidence and there is a good reason for the similarity. Both *Euphorbia* species and cacti have evolved to cope with the same environmental pressures of heat, infrequent and low rainfall, and desiccation. The huge *Euphorbia canariensis* is common as is *Euphorbia balsamifera*, whose stems are much-branched and woody. In Anaga, in the northeast of the island, a ridge of hills rises to 3,360ft (1,021m) and still holds the remnants of the once widespread evergreen laurel forest known locally as 'laurasilva'. The woods are particularly good at Monte de las Mercedes, near La Laguna, and the patient and lucky birdwatcher may still find the long-toed pigeon, a bird which is, sadly, fast approaching extinction, amongst the laurels. Canary holly grows among the laurels, and firecrests can be heard singing their high-pitched song from the tree canopy. With careful searching, the keen botanist can find endemic plants like the shrubby *Bencomia caudata* and *Silene lagunensis* on the forested crags in the area.

Mount Teide

Tenerife is dominated by Mount Teide which, rising to 12,199ft (3,718m) above sea level, is not

A loud call and red beak make the trumpeter finch unmistakable

only the highest peak in the islands but also the highest mountain in Spain. Often shrouded in mist and cloud on its north side and sometimes even capped with snow, the extinct volcano of Mount Teide lies in the centre of the island. Its scenery and wildlife interest is immense and it is now protected within the boundaries of the fascinating Parque Nacional del Teide.

From the rim of the crater, known as Las Cañadas, you can get a wonderful view of the summit which can be reached by cable car or by foot, if you are feeling energetic. Once at the top, the view is magnificent and on a clear day you can see all the Canary Islands stretching off into the distance. In the skies around the summit you may see plain swifts, a small, dark species

PEACE AND QUIET

which is a speciality of the Canaries and Madeira, hawking for insects in the updraughts. From the Parador de las Cañadas you can explore the surrounding scenery and vegetation. It is dominated by shrubby plants such as the fragrant, white-flowered *Spartocytisus supranubius* and the sticky *Adenocarpus viscosus* with its yellow, gorse-like flowers. However, pride of place must go to the immense and majestic viper's bugloss *Echium wildpretii*. The dramatic scenery of Mount Teide provides a perfect setting for its huge spikes of red flowers.

On the descent from the Parador, it is worth exploring any area of Canary pine where you many find canaries, ancestors of the familiar, yellow cagebirds. The pines are also the haunt of the blue chaffinch. These rare birds, found only on the Canaries, have a song which is very similar to the common chaffinch. However, blue chaffinches are larger and the males are a slaty-blue colour. In open, rocky areas, you may come across small parties of barbary partridges, a species which is widespread in north Africa. They are most frequently seen at dawn when the males may be heard calling and, with their distinctive barred flanks and speckled sides to the neck, they are difficult to confuse with any other species.

Gomera and Hierro

At the western extreme of the Canary Islands chain lie the two small islands of Gomera and Hierro. Because of their oceanic position, their humid climate is

The lichen-draped laurel forests of the Canaries have existed for millions of years

quite unlike that of the easterly islands and their peaks are often shrouded in cloud. Gomera is a tiny volcanic cone with its summit almost in the centre of the island. This peak lies at the heart of the Parque Nacional de Garajonay and from the summit, valleys and ravines radiate down towards the sea. The clouds which often prevail on the northern side of the peak have encouraged the development of evergreen forests and the

humidity also favours the epiphytic lichens which festoon the branches of the trees.

The Gomera forests hold the finest stands of laurel in the whole of the Canaries and provide some of the last remaining sites for two of the islands' rarest endemic birds. Both laurel and long-toed pigeons occur here and are entirely dependent upon this habitat. As the woods are felled outside the national parks, the birds become more and more threatened and are getting close to extinction.

The laurel woodlands also hold firecrests, resplendent with their neatly defined eyestripes and fiery crowns. They flit from branch to branch in the tree canopy, while on the woodland floor the cryptic markings of the woodcock make it difficult to spot. The ground vegetation of the evergreen forests is rich with the St John's wort *Hypericum grandiflorum* and bushy figwort *Scrophularia langeana* being conspicuous. Further down the slopes where the leaf canopy opens out, tree heathers, rock roses and canary broom add colour.

Much of the small island of Hierro is completely inaccessible due to the sheer cliffs which rise to a height of 4,900ft (1,500m) at the island's summit. Its semi-circular shape suggests that it is probably part of an extinct volcano, but the slopes are now covered in dense evergreen laurel and pine woodland. The region known as 'El Golfo' is one of the most accessible areas of laurel forest with a colourful woodland floor containing the cranesbill *Geranium canariense*. In open areas the giant spurge *Euphorbia regis-jubae* is common and reaches the height of some of the trees.

La Palma

La Palma still has extensive areas of forest, but the most impressive and best known feature of the island is its volcanic crater. The cone dominates the surrounding landscape, but for best effect it must be viewed from the rim. From the highest point, at nearly 8,000ft (2,500m), you get a panoramic view of the island and you can also look down into the

PEACE AND QUIET

Adenocarpus viscosus is unique to the Canary Islands

crater itself, the Caldera de Taburiente, among the deepest volcanic craters in the world. The outer rim of the crater is heavily wooded and has a wide variety of shrubby legumes. The sticky *Adenocarpus viscosus* and bushy *Spartocytisus supranubius* are common here and are also found in the subalpine zone on Tenerife.

These wild places are a favourite haunt of the aerobatic chough, its finger-like wing-tips in flight and loud 'chough' call making it easy to identify. On the ground it is a bit more ungainly as it probes for insects with its long, red bill.

The northeast region of La Palma is still heavily forested and remains the haunt of both laurel and long-toed pigeons. From an elevated position you may see them flying over the forest canopy below when they look superficially similar to a woodpigeon. However, both species lack the woodpigeon's white wing patches and can be told from one another by the banded tail and speckled neck of the long-toed pigeon.

In the southern tip of La Palma there is a vivid reminder that you are on a volcanic island. The volcano of Teneguía, near Fuencaliente, last erupted as recently as 1971, showering the surrounding land with ash. The tenacity of nature is well illustrated by the plants that have already begun to recolonise the wasted land.

The inhabitants of La Palma successfully manage to cultivate exotic crops like pineapple, avocado and banana in the uninviting soil and after the crops have been harvested, small flocks of birds gather to feed. Trumpeter finches and lesser short-toed larks are sometimes found on the ground, while spectacled warblers skulk in even the lowest bushy scrub around the field margins.

The Islands and their Flora: Origins and Future

The majority of the 2,000 or so species of flowering plants found on the Canaries are endemic to the islands, which means they are not found anywhere else in the world. This is an extraordinary figure and is due in part to the great age of the islands and their lengthy isolation from the mainland of Africa.

Some of the Canaries' plants are widespread throughout the islands while others are distinctly local. The laurels and pines are restricted to small pockets at high altitude on most of the islands. However, at one time they would have been much more widespread on the northern sides of the western islands, and their dwindling range is due to man's activities. Some plants, however, such as the tiny endemic violet, *Viola cheiranthifolia*, have probably never been widespread. This species has probably only ever occurred on the highest slopes of Mount Teide where it still grows today: its restricted distribution is due to its precise habitat needs. The little violet continues to survive but other plants have not fared so well: the charming trailing vetch, *Lotus berthelotii*, is now almost unknown in the wild.

The origin of the islands themselves has obviously had a profound influence on the plants

that are found there today. At one time, the island range was probably connected to Africa, gradually drifting away from the continent. Much of the island landscape has subsequently been affected by violent volcanic activity and some of the western islands are probably entirely volcanic in origin. The Canaries have probably been separated from the mainland since at least the Pliocene, a period in the earth's history, 15–20 million years ago, when the average global temperature dropped significantly. Evergreen laurel forests which once covered the entire Mediterranean and North African region died out throughout most of their range. However, they survived on the Canaries as the islands drifted

This trailing vetch is one of the plants in the Canaries which is threatened by human activity

away from the mainland because of the modifying influence of the ocean – turning the islands into living time capsules.

It is sad to think that the laurels survived on the Canaries for 15 million years until man arrived. What followed is a familiar story: during his brief but devastating residence man has managed to all but wipe out the evergreen forests on many of the islands.

The Distribution of the Canary Flora and Man's Influence

The climate and geology of the Canaries have had a profound influence on the natural distribution of the plants of the islands as well as on the ability to grow crops. Both their oceanic position and the range of altitudes have encouraged a great diversity.

The islands are far from flat and the high altitudes of some have

Walls of cinders help figs and vines grow on Lanzarote

encouraged a series of natural plant 'zones' to develop, each with its own specially adapted plants. These range from the succulents around the coast through the evergreen laurels and pines to subalpine plants near the mountain summits. Man's influence has been most strongly felt around the coasts, but the forests have also suffered as trees were felled for timber and firewood.

Were it not for their oceanic position and prevailing trade winds, which moderate the extremes in temperature, the Canaries would have a Mediterranean-type climate with hot, dry summers and mild, wet winters. As it is, the moisture-laden northeasterly winds create almost permanent cloud-cover on the mountains, allowing evergreen trees to survive. Despite the volcanic soil, considerable success has been achieved in cultivating plants on the Canaries. Over the years, the crops grown have reflected

changing needs, so at one time the ice plant,
Mesembryanthemum crystallinum, was grown for soda extraction. This was then replaced by prickly pears, new-world cacti, grown not for their own sake, but in order to feed the cochineal bugs which yielded cochineal dye. Nowadays, much of the Canaries' agriculture is geared to supplying market garden vegetables and fruit for export, and tomatoes, potatoes and even bananas all thrive in the arid soil. The mild winters ensure that crops can be harvested earlier than in northern Europe and some are picked all year round. Considerable ingenuity has been necessary to get the most out of the harsh environment. There is little standing water so, instead, bore-holes in the mountainsides pipe it into reservoirs for irrigation. The wind is often harsh, especially the drying Saharan winds felt on Lanzarote. For protection, the plants are often grown in little hollows surrounded by lava and cinder walls and these also collect any rain that falls. As a result, vines and even fig trees are grown successfully.

Seabirds

The seas surrounding the Canary Islands are rich in marine life and large numbers of seabirds gather to feed on this bounty. Some of them breed around the islands and are present for most of the year, while others are visitors from all over the world.
Seabirds are often seen from the islands themselves. Almost

Sabine's gull is one of the most elegant seabirds

invariably, dawn and dusk are the best times of day, and an onshore breeze will certainly improve your chances. However, boat trips and inter-island ferries provide the best opportunities for watching the birds, often giving exceptionally close views.
The most frequently seen species around the coast of the Canaries is Cory's shearwater. These large, brown birds fly with stiff wings, banking and gliding low over the water's surface. During strong winds, however, they often soar to great heights and make the best possible use of every gust and updraught.
Cory's shearwaters are often joined by their diminutive relative, the little shearwater, which with its fluttering flight looks more like a puffin than a shearwater. Both little shearwaters and Bulwer's petrels, another speciality of the

PEACE AND QUIET

islands, breed on the offshore islets of Graciosa and Montaña Clara off Lanzarote.

During the later summer and autumn, the resident seabird numbers are swollen by migrant species. Great and sooty shearwaters are visitors from their south Atlantic breeding colonies, while from August onwards, Sabine's gulls become common. These most elegant of seabirds breed in the brief summers of the high Arctic, abandoning their breeding grounds before many other species have even finished nesting.

On any of the longer ferry trips you may see small, black seabirds with white rumps, following the boats. These are storm petrels, and several different species occur in the waters off the Canaries. Madeiran petrels breed on the

nearby Madeiran islands and are found throughout the year. However, from May until October you can also find Wilson's petrels, visitors from the Antarctic. Although the two species are superficially similar, Wilson's petrels have longer legs and yellow feet with which they patter over the surface of the water.

Cochineal Bugs

Before the advent of modern synthetic chemicals, all dyes had natural origins and some of them came from most unlikely sources such as lichens, soil sediments and tree bark. However, there could have been no more peculiar a source than that for cochineal, which was the dried bodies of a special kind of bug. Cochineal is a dye which was, and to some extent still is, used to stain fibres red. Its source is the cochineal bug Dactylopius coccus, which thrives on prickly pear, and both of these were introduced to the Canaries from Mexico. The dye was so important to the economy of the islands that fields of the cactus were planted to support huge numbers of bugs.

Nowadays, a variety of synthetic dyes has largely replaced cochineal and the prickly pear fields have consequently fallen into disuse. However, these hardy cacti thrive on neglect and colonies of bugs, with their characteristic mealy appearance, can still be found on the islands.

Cochineal bugs and prickly pears were introduced from Mexico

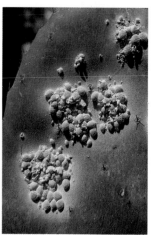

FOOD AND DRINK

There is a great variety of food
and drink in the Canary Islands,
with most European nations
represented, including, of
course, Spain. The Canaries
also have many regional
specialities, all relying on local
produce. Some Canarian
favourites: *Mojo sauce*, used
everywhere as an
accompaniment to fish and meat
dishes, is the most distinctive
element of Canarian eating.
Green mojo – *mojo verde* – is
based on parsley and coriander.
Red mojo is based on sweet red
pepper but may be spiked with
chilli. It can be hot – taste
cautiously before applying.
There are many other mojo
sauces, some very complicated.
Sancocho is a rich fish stew,
generally of sea bass or salt
cod, poached with sweet
potatoes and served with mojo
sauce.
Gofio is a roasted, powdered
cereal made up in various ways.
It can be used to make a bread
substitute; like flour, it will
thicken soups and gravies; it is
also sprinkled over food.
Papas arrugadas – wrinkled
potatoes – are salty potatoes
boiled in their skins.
Rich soups full of bits and
pieces, amounting almost to
stew, are very popular.
Canarian *potaje* is a vegetable,
or meat-and-veg, first course
broth using local produce.
Canarians particularly enjoy
pork and rabbit. Fresh fish is
excellent.
Puddings are not to be missed.
Try *Bien me sabe* – literally,
'How good it tastes' – with real

*A café in Los Cristianos, Tenerife,
where it's always the season for
eating out of doors*

honey, almonds and a dash of
rum. (When Canarians say *miel*
– honey in Spanish – they
generally mean cane syrup.)
Frangollo is made with gofio
and raisins, liberally covered in
'honey'. Bananas are cooked all
kinds of ways, often flambé, and
flan – or caramel pudding – is
as popular as on the Spanish
mainland.

Drink
Local wines are found
throughout the islands, some
better than others. Lanzarote's
speciality is *Malvasia*, or
Malmsey. **Water** – drink bottled
where possible.

SHOPPING

The Canary Islands have long enjoyed free port status. Though not always competitive, they are worth considering for the kind of articles normally found in duty free shops at airports, and for electronic goods. There is also attractive local produce on the larger islands. Suggestions are given for each island individually.

ACCOMMODATION

The major resorts have many large hotels, generally modern and comfortable, with all the facilities that might be expected in seaside resorts – swimming pools, evening entertainment, hairdressing... and so on. Some resorts, particularly in Gran Canaria (Las Palmas), also have numerous apartment hotels or 'aparthotels'. These are similar to regular hotels (with facilities like full dining-room service) but also have small kitchens for each room or suite, and probably a food shop on the premises as well. The smaller islands have smaller hotels. Most of the islands also offer 'paradors'. These are hotels belonging to Spain's excellent state-run chain, usually in interesting, sometimes isolated positions and frequently in beautiful buildings, old or new. There are few pensions (full-board only) in the Canaries; small inland towns and fishing villages are the best places to search these out.

In some islands, particularly Lanzarote, villas are available through tour operators. They are generally well fitted out. In recent years, time-share apartments have been increasing in number. They have often been aggressively marketed and may present difficulties in maintenance. Their value does not always increase as expected and to look at they are often a dense carpet of low-rise estates.

The palm garden and pool of the Los Fariones 4-star hotel, Puerto del Carmen, Lanzarote

CULTURE, ENTERTAINMENT AND NIGHTLIFE

See individual islands.

WEATHER AND WHEN TO GO

For most European countries, particularly Scandinavia and Germany, the 'season' for the Canaries is winter. It is generally warm enough to swim and to get a good sun-tan. The British tend to visit the Canaries all year round. A word of warning, though, to accompany the favourable sunshine statistics. The northern sides of almost all the islands are rainier than the south – because this is where the cloud-forming, moisture-bearing trade winds first make contact. Northern resorts can be quite wet and the whole of an island may be overcast for days in a row. Winds can be strong the whole year round. This being said, the climate is on the whole admirable, and claims of a year-round springtime are by no means far-fetched.

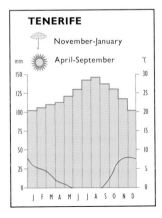

TENERIFE

November-January

April-September

HOW TO BE A LOCAL

Canarian people are friendly but a little reserved compared with mainland Spaniards. Visitors will be doing everyone a favour if they do not yell and shout too much. English and German are widely spoken on the larger islands but a few words of Spanish and a friendly smile will work wonders on the smaller ones. On the latter particularly, do not be afraid of scruffy-looking bars and restaurants, to a Canarian, it is the quality of the food rather than the decor which distinguishes the best eating places. Food is often good and service friendly, not to say heartwarming. And this, of course, is where you find the locals. Sunday lunch is an occasion for eating out with friends and family when the atmosphere in many restaurants resembles a fiesta. *Do* pick up hitchhikers particularly on the smaller islands. Public transport is often minimal and leaving people by the roadside is regarded as discourteous. Codes of dress and behaviour among Canarians tend to be conservative, even formal, but within the tourist resorts practically anything goes. There is a well-established gay scene in Las Palmas, Gran Canaria and in the southern resorts of Tenerife.

Although the islands are small, there is a very clear distinction between tourist lifestyle and traditional island ways. This is part of the charm of the Canaries. The visitor who respects this distinction will certainly enjoy the best of both worlds.

Carnival at Las Palmas

CHILDREN

The Canaries offer a lot for children in terms of climate and general facilities. For particular venues, see individual islands.

TIGHT BUDGET

● A good saving can be made by booking holidays at the very last minute.
● You rarely have to pay an entrance fee to get into a disco.
● The 'menu of the day' often works out cheaper than snacks.
● Choose local beer rather than imported brands; though local wine is more expensive.
● The Tenerife and Gran Canaria bus services are cheap and reliable.
● Use public call boxes – much cheaper than hotel phones.
● It makes sense to shop where the locals shop. Most items are cheaper in ordinary shops than at the airport duty-free shop.

● Gomero or Hierro are beautiful and there's little opportunity to take out your wallet while there.

SPECIAL EVENTS

Carnival is a major affair, usually in late February or early March. So, in several islands, is Corpus Christi in June. For major events, see individual islands.

SPORT

There is plenty to choose from; some pointers are given under individual island entries. There are also some homegrown sports, notably the very popular Canarian wrestling, *lucha Canaria,* deriving directly from the original Guanche inhabitants. This is a gentlemanly team affair requiring agility and balance rather than brute strength. Newspapers give venues. There is another Guanche survival, the *Juego del Palo* or 'stick game', a kind of quarter-stave combat akin to fencing.

DIRECTORY

Contents

Arriving

By air

Tenerife, Gran Canaria (Las Palmas), Lanzarote and Fuerteventura can all be reached direct from many airports in Western Europe, Africa and North America either by scheduled airline, charter flight or both. All the islands except Gomera (an airport is under construction), can be reached on inter-island flights. The airport on Gran Canaria is named Gando, 12½ miles (20km) south of Las Palmas. The airport bus to Las Palmas leaves every 30 minutes. A public bus service to the city runs every 15 minutes. Tenerife has two airports, the large and modern Reina Sofía airport in the south, already needing expansion, and Los Rodeos in the north, now used mainly for inter-island flights. In 1977, Los Rodeos was the scene of one of aviation's worst disasters, caused by the collision of two jumbo jets; this and the rapid growth of tourism lay behind the decision to build a new airport in the south. Here there is a better approach and generally better weather conditions. There are no special problems associated with any of the other international airports.

By sea

The islands can be reached by regular services from Cádiz on the Spanish mainland to Santa Cruz (Tenerife), Las Palmas (Gran Canaria) and Arrecife (Lanzarote), so those coming for long periods can bring their own vehicles, but be prepared for a two-day voyage. Consult the Spanish Tourist Office for details of services.

Camping

Only Tenerife and Gran Canaria have official camp sites but nobody objects if the odd tent goes up. However, you cannot camp in a national park without official permission. Consult tourist office. Caves, once used by the Guanches, are a good alternative.

DIRECTORY

Chemist
See **Pharmacist**

Crime
In the smaller islands there is no cause for concern but in cities like Las Palmas it is advisable to keep an eye on your belongings and your person, at certain times and in certain places. Remember to keep your car locked and your belongings in the boot. Most hotels have safe deposit facilities which you would do well to use.

Customs Regulations
Although there are limits to the amount of alcohol, cigarettes, tobacco and the like which can be imported into mainland Spain, these regulations do not apply to the Canary Islands, where there are no restrictions on imported or exported goods. Nevertheless, you will not necessarily find that prices are very low as a consequence; shops have a tendency to put up their own prices, and not every purchase is a bargain – except for drinks, which are remarkably cheap, and tobacco, which is a local product.

Driving
● Car Hire
Although official regulations state you must have an international licence or a full Spanish translation of your national licence, in practice all valid British, European, American and Australian licences are acceptable. There are plenty of car hire firms in all the islands, usually with unlimited mileage. Prices vary considerably between large hire companies and small local firms: shop

Vilaflor, one of the picturesque villages of Tenerife

around, keeping in mind that this may reflect genuinely competitive rates or hazardous corner-cutting in maintenance. In the event of breakdown or accident, telephone the local office of your car hire firm and be sure to follow the instructions given in your rental documentation.

The same rules apply as in Spain and the rest of mainland Europe – drive on the right, overtake on the left and give way to traffic approaching from the right unless there are contrary signs.

Use of seat belts is compulsory except in towns. Children under

10 must travel in the back of the car.

In towns, cars must be parked facing the same direction as movement of traffic.

● Documents

Most visitors to the Canaries use hire cars. For those who plan a longer stay and wish to take their own car, you would be well advised to consult the Spanish Tourist Office or motoring associations. Spain has some notable peculiarities, such as the requirement for a bail bond in case of accident.

● Petrol

Careful – petrol stations may well be closed on Sundays. They rarely accept credit cards.

● Speed Limits

Motorways 120kph (74mph).
Roads with two or more lanes in each direction 100kph (62mph)
Built-up areas 60kph (37mph).

Electricity

Normally 220 volts although many hotels have 100 volt. Sockets accept two round-pin type plugs. Two-pronged round pin plug for electric shavers, though the prongs do not match the British type and an adaptor is required.

Embassies and Consulates

Las Palmas, Gran Canaria
United Kingdom Calle Luis Morote, 6 (tel: 26 25 08)
US Calle José Franchy Roca, 5 (tel: 27 12 59).

Tenerife
United Kingdom Calle de Suárez Guerra, 40 Santa Cruz de Tenerife (tel: 24 20 00).

Emergency Telephone Numbers

Police (all islands): 091 (emergencies only).

Province of Tenerife
Red cross (Cruz Roja): 28 29 24
Ambulance service: 28 18 00
Fire service: (Tenerife, Santa Cruz) 22 00 80; (Tenerife, Puerto de la Cruz) 33 00 80; (La Palma) 41 11 50.

Province of Gran Canaria
Red Cross: 23 00 00
Ambulance service: 24 59 21
Fire service: (Gran Canaria) 20 71 22; (Lanzarote) 81 48 58.

Entertainment Information

Available from your hotel reception, tourist information office, local press and, most reliably, by word of mouth (see **Media**).

DIRECTORY

Entry Formalities

A valid passport, but no visa, is required by citizens of the UK, the US, Canada, Australia and New Zealand for stays of up to three months. For UK citizens, a British Visitor's Passport is acceptable. To extend your stay, apply to police authorities. No paid work is allowed during this time.

Health Regulations

No special vaccinations are required.

Health Care

Similar to mainland Spain. Standards are generally acceptable. Most doctors speak and understand some English.

Intricate embroidery is a local speciality

Citizens of EC states are eligible for free medical and hospital treatment and pay only for dental treatment and prescribed medicines. (This involves obtaining Form E111 for UK travellers, before leaving home; if needed, it should be presented to the local office of the Instituto de la Seguridad Social.) Short-stay visitors should also take out some form of independent insurance cover. Non-EC nationals should always take out private insurance.

Holidays

Fixed Dates

1 January – Año Nuevo (New Year's Day)
6 January – Los Reyes (Epiphany)
2 February – La Candelaria (Candlemass)
19 March – San José (St Joseph's Day)
1 May – Día del Trabajo (Labour Day)
25 July – Santiago (St James's Day)
15 August – Asunción (Assumption)
12 October – Día de la Hispanidad (Discovery of America, Columbus Day)
1 November – Todos los Santos (All Saints)
8 December – Immaculáda Concepción (Immaculate Conception)
25 December – Navidad (Christmas)

Moveable Feasts

Jueves Santo (Maundy Thursday)
Viernes Santo (Good Friday)
Pascua (Easter)
Lunes de Pascua (Easter Monday)
Corpus Christi (May/June)

Lost Property

Report details to Municipal Police or Guardia Civil (see **Police** for phone numbers).

Media

Television programmes are in Spanish and most of them are relayed from the mainland. BBC World Service and Voice of America can be picked up on short wave radio. Local radio stations in Las Palmas and Tenerife broadcast short news and music programmes in English daily. *Here and Now* is an English language paper published fortnightly under the slogan 'The Canary Islands' Only English Newspaper', by *Diario de Avisos*. English language magazines include *Island Gazette,* a monthly publication. There is also the bi-monthly *Canarias Tourist.* Most of the larger islands have their own publications such as the monthly *Tenerife Leisure Scene.* There are also various property publications. BBC TV news, in English, is broadcast nightly on Channel 2, generally rather late. Check times locally.

Money Matters

The unit of currency, as on mainland Spain, is the peseta (pta). There are 1,000, 2,000, 5,000 and 10,000-peseta banknotes and 1, 5, 10, 25, 50, 100, 200 and 500-peseta coins. Banks are open weekdays 09.00–14.00hrs, Saturdays 09.00–13.00hrs, closed Sundays. All banks accept major credit cards – American Express, Diners Club, Access, Eurocard, Visa. You can change money at banks, exchange offices and larger hotels. The commission varies. British National Girobank account holders can withdraw money from post offices in the main resorts.

Credit Cards

Larger hotels, classier restaurants, banks, major shops and car rental firms will accept all major credit cards. Petrol stations normally will not.

Opening Times
Offices

Usually Monday to Friday 09.00–13.00hrs and 15.00–19.00hrs; Saturday 09.00–13.00hrs.

Shops

Usually 09.00–13.00hrs and 16.00–20.00hrs, Saturday 09.00–13.00hrs. But this may vary. For museum opening times, consult individual entries.

Personal Safety

Children particularly should be protected from sunburn. Always take water, extra clothing and wear stout shoes or boots on any expedition at high altitude, for instance on Mount Teide in Tenerife, or where the weather is likely to be changeable.

Pharmacist

Open: normal shopping hours Monday to Friday 09.00–13.00hrs; 16.00–20.00hrs, Saturday 09.00–13.00hrs. Identified by the word **Farmacia** and a green cross shop sign. Each pharmacy should display the address of the nearest duty pharmacy of **Farmacia de Guardia** open outside these hours. After 22.00hrs only medicines on prescription are issued. Some medicines requiring a prescription in other

DIRECTORY

countries are sold across the counter in Spain. Shops called *droguerías* sell cosmetics, not drugs or medicines.

Places of Worship

Spanish churches are normally Roman Catholic. Visitors are very welcome to attend their services.

Church of England services are held at All Saints Church, Taoro Park, Puerto de la Cruz, Tenerife (vicar, tel: 38 40 38), and Holy Trinity Church, corner of Calle Brasil and Calle Rafael Ramirez, Las Palmas, Gran Canaria (chaplain's residence, tel: 25 72 02). The Templo Ecuménico near the Kasbah precinct, Playa del Inglés, holds services for different denominations in turn.

Police

There are three different police forces. The **Policía Municipal** (Municipal Police) in blue uniform and cap, have responsibility for traffic. The **Policía Nacional** wear brown and berets and are in charge of crime control. The **Guardia Civil** (Civil Guard) in pea-green uniform and cap or sometimes in distinctive black patent leather tricorn hat, are responsible for coasts and customs, rural areas and highway patrol.

The emergency number which can be dialled to reach police in all islands is: 091.

Policía Municipal

Tenerife Santa Cruz tel: 092; Puerto de la Cruz tel: 38 04 28
Gomera tel: 87 00 62
Hierro tel: 55 0025
Gran Canaria Las Palmas tel: 092; San Augustín tel: 76 24 12
Fuerteventura tel: 85 06 35

Lanzarote tel: 81 13 17

Post Office

Post and Telegraph offices (**Correos y Telégrafos**) open Monday to Friday 09.00–14.00hrs, Saturday 09.00–13.00hrs. You cannot telephone from a post office but you can send a telegram – or dictate one by telephone, tel: 22 20 00. See also **Telephones**. Spanish post boxes are yellow. All mail leaves the Canaries by air and normally takes 5 days to reach northern European addresses. Stamps available at most tobacconists and shops selling post cards as well as at post offices.

Public Transport
● Air

All islands except Gomera have an airport and are connected by inter-island flights. flights between Tenerife and Gran Canaria are almost hourly. These are well-used by islanders; early booking is advisable.

● Ferries

All islands can be reached by ferries, mostly run by the Compañía Trasmediterránea. There is an additional jetfoil service between Las Palmas (Gran Canaria) and Santa Cruz (Tenerife) and from both to Morro Jable (Fuerteventura). Gomera is reached by ferry or hydrofoil from Los Cristianos on Tenerife (35 minutes by hydrofoil).

● Buses

Buses are a good way of getting about on Tenerife and Gran Canaria where the services are frequent and reliable. The smaller islands are rather less well served and, on these,

Playa Calera is one of Gomera's few beaches. It lies at the end of Valle Gran Rey

hitchhiking is a common method of transport. Magnetic stored-value 'bond' tickets give a 40 per cent discount on cash fares and can be bought at TITSA offices or some banks.

● **Taxis**
Identified by the letters SP on the front and rear of a car, standing for 'servicio público'. Most are metered at a rate fixed by the municipal authorities. There are usually fixed rates for long distances. Confirm the fare before beginning the journey.

Senior Citizens
The winter climate of the Canaries is ideal for, and much enjoyed by, senior citizens. Facilities are generally modern and standards of comfort high.

Student and Youth Travel
There are no youth hostels in the Canaries.

Telephones
Each province has its own code: **922** for Tenerife, Gomera, Hierro and La Palma; **928** for Gran Canaria, Lanzarote and Fuerteventura. When calling from one province to another, use the full code and then dial the number required. When calling inside a province simply dial the number, not the code.

Codes to the Canaries
Dial 010–34, then the provincial code, omitting the initial 9. For the province of Tenerife dial 010–34–22 then the number; for Gran Canaria, Lanzarote and Fuerteventura, dial 010–34–28 then the number.

Codes from the Canaries
Dial the country code (UK

DIRECTORY

07–44; Eire 07–353; US and Canada 07–1; Australia 07–61; New Zealand 07–64); then the local code, omitting the initial zero; then the number.

Public Telephones
Instructions show you how to place your coins in the machine so that they roll down as needed. Dialling as above.

Time (local)
Normally as in Britain. Briefly out of step, however, owing to different dates of start/end of summer/winter time. Five hours ahead of American Eastern Standard Time; 10 hours behind South Australia and 12 hours behind New Zealand.

Tipping
Most bills have service charge included but it is customary to leave an extra 5 per cent or so, or at least the small change.

Toilets
Public toilets are rare. The wise remember to use the facilities in the restaurants and bars they patronise. If you are desperate, no barman will mind if you pop in and ask to use the toilet.

Tourist Offices
United Kingdom
Spanish National Tourist Office, 57–8 St James's Street, London SW1A 1LD (tel: 071 499 0901).

US
Spanish National Tourist Office, 665 Fifth Avenue, New York NY 10022 (tel: (212) 759 8822).

Canada
Spanish National Tourist Office, 102 Bloor Street West, 14th floor Toronto, Ontario M5S 1M8 (tel: (416) 961 3131).

Tenerife
Playa de las Américas by Pueblo Canaria, opposite Gran Tinerfe Hotel
Puerto de la Cruz Plaza de la Iglésia 3 (tel: 38 43 28/37 19 28).
Santa Cruz Palacio Insular, Plaza de España (tel: 24 22 27).

Gomera
For tourist information apply to the Island Council, Cabildo Insular, Calle General Franco 20, San Sebastián (tel: 87 01 03).

Hierro
Tourist Information Office, Calle Dr Quintero 11, Valverde (tel: 55 03 02).

La Palma
Officina de Turismo, Calle O'Daly 6, Santa Cruz (tel: 41 21 06).

Gran Canaria
Las Palmas Casa del Turismo, Parque Santa Catalina (tel: 26 46 23), and Patronato Insular de Turismo, Calle León y Castillo 17 (tel: 36 22 22).

Fuerteventura
Cabildo Insular, Calle Rosario 7, Puerto del Rosario (tel: 85 14 00).

Lanzarote
Officina de Turismo, Parque Municipal, Arrecife (tel: 81 18 60).

Travel Agencies
Many tour operators are linked to wholly or partly owned Spanish subsidiaries. If you are on a package holiday, your representative will make it clear which local company is organised to help you. Viajes Canyrama, operating in many of the islands, head office Las Palmas, Gran Canaria (tel: 27 65 53), has a good reputation.

LANGUAGE

yes sí
no no
please por favor
thank you gracias
good morning buenos días
good night buenas noches
I want quiero
I am looking for busco
where is? ¿dónde está?
how much? ¿cuanto es?
airport aeropuerto
beach playa
hotel hotel
restaurant restaurante
beer cerveza
milk leche
water agua
wine vino
bread pan
fish pescado
fruit fruta
meat carne
pudding postre

can I have? ¿me da?
chemist una farmacia
doctor el médico
expensive caro
help ayuda
hospital hospital
I've lost my... he perdido mi...
luggage equipaje
map un mapa
market un mercado
mineral water agua mineral
name el nombre
newspaper un periódico
night noche
number número
pardon? ¿cómo?
passport pasaporte
police la policía
postcard una postal
stamp un sello
room la habitación
shower ducha
suitcase una maleta

La Palma's volcanic crater

INDEX

INDEX/ACKNOWLEDGEMENTS

ACKNOWLEDGEMENTS

The Automobile Association
would like to thank the following
photographers and libraries for
their assistance in the
compilation of this book:
J ALLAN CASH PHOTO LIBRARY
5 Windmill, 8 Farming nr.
Agaete, 9 Teide's crater, 13 Los
Cristianos, 14 Los Gigantes, 19
Candelaria, 26 Loro Parque, 29
Flower market, Santa Cruz, 31
Gomera, Valle Gran Rey, 37
Vallehermoso, 39 El Golfo, 42/3
Roques de Salmór, 45 Santa
Cruz, 48 Ayuntamiento, Santa
Cruz, 50/1 San Antonio,
Fuencaliente, 52 Caldera de
Taburiente, 55 Caldera de
Taburiente, 57 Puerto Rico, 60/1
Playa del Inglés, 66 Doramas
Park, Las Palmas, 68/9 View from
Cruz de Tejeda, 70 Palmitos
Parque, 74 Folk Dancing, 76
Golfing, 77 Windmill,
Fuerteventura, 80 Fuerteventura,
83 Pájara, 90/1 Puerto del
Carmen, 93 Arrecife, 94
Towards Haría, 97 Camel rides,
113 Los Cristianos, 116 Carnival,
120 Embroidery, 123 Playa
Calera, 125 La Palma's crater.
A HOPKINS 20 Dragon Tree, 35
El Cercado, 36 Valle Gran Rey,
85 Windsurfing, 88 Timanfaya,
114 Palm Garden.
GABRIELLE MACPHEDRAN 41
The Ermita of La Dehesa.
INTERNATIONAL PHOTOBANK
Cover Tenerife, 18 Santa Cruz,
22 Valle de la Orotava, 24/5
Caldera de Las Cañadas, 62
Maspalomas, 118/9 Vilaflor.
NATURE PHOTOGRAPHERS
LTD 101 Wildpretii (B Burbidge),
102 Senecio kleinia (K J Carlson),
104 Euphorbia Canariensis (B
Burbidge), 105 Trumpeter finch
(R Tidman), 106/7 Laurel forest
(B Burbidge), 108 Adenocarpus
viscosus (B Burbidge), 109
Trailing vetch (B Burbidge), 110
Fig Tree (N A Callow), 111
Sabine's gull (D Goodfellow),
112 Cochineal bug (S C Bisserot).